CAROLYN LEWIS was born in Cardiff an
1987. She is married with three daug
seven grandchildren. Carolyn has been
old. After leaving school, she trained as a journalist for the South Wales
Echo and Western Mail, leaving to have her children.

Returning to work, she became a press officer for a number of
organisations including Mencap. During this time, she began writing short
stories, winning a number of prizes and awards. She co-founded a women
only writing group which ran successfully for five years.

In 1993, following major spinal surgery, Carolyn embarked on a
part-time English degree course at the University of the West of England,
attaining a 2:1. In 1999, immediately following graduation, she applied
and was accepted on an MPhil in Writing at the University of Glamorgan.
Since her graduation, she has taught creative writing, taking workshops
into local schools, adult education centres and has also worked for a drug
rehabilitation project in Bath. Her novel *Missing Nancy* was written as part
of the MPhil, and was published in 2008 by Accent Press. She also writes
short stories for *Woman's Weekly*.

Published in paperback by SilverWood Books 2010
www.silverwoodbooks.co.uk
This book is a SilverWood Original – traditional publishing at its best

ISBN 978-1-906236-18-2

British Library Cataloguing in Publication Data
A CIP catalogue record for this book is available
from the British Library

Set in Trade Gothic by SilverWood Books
Printed in England by Berforts Group, Stevenage Herts SG1 2BH

THE
NOVEL
A Perfect Recipe

Carolyn Lewis

SilverWood
originals

Other titles from SilverWood Originals

Memories of a PierMaster's Mistress
by Maggie Ashford
ISBN 9781906236083
The story of the restoration of Clevedon Pier

Introduction

Beginnings

Introduction

There are many good books on novel writing and you may feel that this is simply another one, no different from the rest. But I hope you'll find that this one *is* different – because what I've aimed to do with this book is to demystify the art of novel writing, to present it in bite-sized chunks, to make it achievable for new novelists. I can't teach you how to write, I can't give you that particular talent, but what I can offer is to guide you through the novel writing process, to show you how to avoid the pitfalls, and to encourage you to complete a novel. I've taught creative writing for almost twenty years and these are some of the methods I've used with my students.

Carolyn Lewis BA(Hons), MPhil in Writing

Beginnings

Why do you want to write…? Do you have an idea for a novel? A particular character you want to write about? Something that keeps you awake at night?

Perhaps writing is something you've wanted to do for a long time but you've kept quiet about it? Maybe you've started to write a novel many times before, but have yet to complete it? Or perhaps it's none of these things. Writing is something you think you can do, and the reason you haven't is simple – you're not sure how to begin.

Novice writers often believe there is a magic formula, some kind of trick they need to master before they can start writing. There is no such thing, no secret society to join.

* It's about you finding the **determination** to begin.
* It's about getting the **tools** you'll need: a pen, notebook and perhaps a PC or a laptop.
* And, of course, it's about finding the **time**.

Armed with these things, the final step is simple: make yourself sit down and write.

1

Get A Writing Habit

How do I start?
A writing habit
A reading habit
What kind of writer are you?

As a creative writing tutor, new students often come to me and say, "I want to write…but what do I need to do? What should I be writing about? How do I start?"

My answer is always the same. "Try to write something every day. Whether it's one sentence or a thousand, get into a 'writing habit'. Make time for your writing, factor it into your day, every day."

Facing a blank screen or an empty page is daunting so all new and aspiring writers (and quite a few seasoned ones!) need to have something to write about.

One of the exercises I use to kick-start my students into writing mode is to describe a room that has some importance to them. It might be a bedroom…it might be the room that your grandmother sat in…it might be the room where you were offered your first job. Write about the colour of the carpet, and whether there are pictures on the wall. Is there a smell associated with this room? Does it have wide windows with a view overlooking a park? Go into great detail, see what you can remember. Don't stop your pen moving, keep going. As one memory comes back, others will too.

When you've exhausted the possibilities offered by a room, move on to something else that is of importance to you. Your first day at school. Your graduation day. Your wedding day. Don't worry about the quality of your writing at this stage, just get the words down on paper; bear in mind that these are beginnings and they don't have to suit anyone else, only you.

Tell yourself that you'll write for half an hour and then stop. The next day, write for a little longer.

While you're getting your writing habit started, I recommend that you get a reading habit started too. Stephen King said that there are two things to do if you want to be a writer. The first is to read a lot, the second is to write a lot. I firmly believe that if you don't read, you can't write. So read everything you can lay your hands on. Read good novels, bad novels, novels that are bestsellers. Read again the novels you have enjoyed and explore the reasons for that enjoyment. Observe the way that other writers go about their craft. Look at the way they handle dialogue, how they build their characters, how the pace and plot of the novel is achieved. Make notes so you have a record of your findings that you can go back to if necessary.

Work out what you like in the good novels, and what you don't like in the bad novels. See if you can spot what makes a bestseller! I find it interesting that, having told my students that I want them to read as many books as possible, after a while, they tell me that they are reading books in a different frame of mind. It's not that they're being overly critical of novels – they are reading with heightened awareness, with an understanding of what it takes to write a novel.

Observational skills are also important to any writer. Carry a small notebook with you and listen to what's going on around you, wherever you are. Watch people carefully, look for the bizarre, the unusual and write down what you see, what you think you may be able to use. And also remember that the usual, the ordinary has its place in describing a scene and establishing authenticity. George Orwell wrote 'the best books…are those that tell you what you know already'.

Observe the way that other writers go about their craft.

Now you have a writing habit, and hopefully you have a reading habit too. So how to start your novel?

There are many tips and suggestions for the new writer. It may be that ideas are jumping around inside your head, characters keep wandering in and out, making their presence felt and you are not sure how to start writing about them. It might be that you've mapped out the entire novel but fight shy of picking up your pen. Well, sometimes you just have to start. Pick up your pen and paper, or sit down at your PC, and put some words on a page. You might be surprised at the way your writing habit has prepared you; you may find words just keep coming.

But if that doesn't happen, don't worry. Maybe you just need to find out what sort of writer you are…

▪ The METICULOUS writer

If you're a meticulous writer, you may have the entire novel worked out in your head. You will know every nuance of each character, you know exactly what will happen in each chapter and have already decided on the ending.

▪ Got the IDEA, but will go with the flow writer

Are you a writer with ideas or a plot that you've been thinking about for some time? For you, your novel will take shape as you begin to write, testing out your theme, seeing where your ideas take you.

- **A writer with a CHARACTER in mind**

If you are, you'll begin with a character study and then you'll place your characters in different settings and circumstances and then write about the way they react to the situations you've put them in.

- **A writer who lets their FINGERS do the walking**

This writer will simply sit down and begin to write, seeing what they can achieve, writing with no conscious theme, just letting the pen or the keyboard do all the work.

■ EXERCISE

If you're a meticulous writer, try writing down the outline of your novel, making numbered headings. Perhaps you start with a shooting or a murder – that will be your number one heading. Work your way through to number ten or maybe twenty as you proceed through the plot of your novel. If you know how your novel will end, that is number twenty. If you know how it begins, if you are writing about a murder, that is number one. You might want to use your numbers as potential chapters: chapter one is the shooting, chapter two is the aftermath of the crime, the effect upon others. Chapter three is the investigation and so on. Your last number, your number twenty, is the culprit being caught or perhaps making his escape. By doing this, you've given yourself a Twenty Point Plan to work on and you can always flesh it out as you work your way through your list.

2

Characters

Finding your characters
Naming your characters
A life of their own
Archetypes and stereotypes

Where do you find characters? Perhaps you've already got one that you've been thinking about for some time. Characters can be an amalgamation of real people – people you know or people you've heard about. They can also be built from half-remembered gestures of someone you once saw behind a till; the voice might come from the man who came to repair your washing machine.

It can be difficult to create a character solely from your imagination because you run the risk of developing a lifeless character who is merely an extension of your own viewpoint. I firmly believe that what you need to do when building your characters is to be very watchful. Develop your observational skills! Watch people: look at what the people around you are doing, follow their movements, look for the out of the ordinary. Look at the ordinary and listen out for the unusual pitch of voice. Listen for the difference in intonation, the raised voice, the placatory voice.

Observe the way that people walk, how they use their hands when talking. How do couples interact? Is there a lot of eye contact? Study their body language and their clothes. Use all these details when writing about a character.

The author William Faulkner says "A writer needs three things – experience, observation and imagination, any two of which, at times any one of which, can supply the lack of the others."

One of the most heady things about writing fiction is inventing characters whose identities come to life on the page, ideally on their own. A well-drawn character is believable, recognisable and easily identifiable with.

To find character names, trawl the Internet. This is an extremely good tool to use, particularly if you're looking for foreign or unusual names.

When I'm working on a character, I begin by naming them. Names are extremely important as they will help identify the age of your character.

Names, like most other things, come in and out of fashion. If your character is an elderly man, you need to choose a name suitable for his age. Even with today's trend for unusual names, an elderly woman is far more likely to have a name like Edna than Kylie. Search through newspapers, raid the obituary columns until you find names that will suit your characters.

Once you've decided on a name, add more detail to cement your character sketch. Write down as many things as possible about your character: their age, their height, whether they are married or not.

If you get stuck, try running through the following list:

- Are they tall?
- Are they slender?
- What job do they do?
- What radio station do they listen to?
- What do they eat for breakfast?
- How often do they have a haircut?
- Where do they go on holiday?
- Are they fastidious?
- Are they careful with their appearance?
- Are they creatures of habit?
- Do they have any children?
- What car do they drive?
- What do they do for a living?
- What newspaper do they read?

Do this for all your main characters; learn everything there is to know about them. You may not use all the information you've written but the object of this exercise is for you to know their likes and dislikes, habits and personality traits. You're searching for the essence of your character, an understanding of the sort of person they are and the way they will behave in any given situation.

Character development is not just about making a character believable, it's also about charting their progress, discovering what they want from life, how they handle whatever comes their way. As writers we should be asking of our characters, "How would they cope with this?" "What will happen to them?" Often a character will grow and, if they grow a lot and take on a life of their own, they can begin to influence the plot of your novel.

Another way to look at the process of building your characters is that you'll learn their strengths and weaknesses as you get to know them. With this knowledge comes the ability to judge how they'll behave in the novel, how they'll cope with whatever you, as writer, throw at them and how their actions will move the novel forward.

You might also find it helpful to write your character's back story. By that, I mean the things they did, the life that they had before they arrived in the novel. Were they head boy at school? Did they go to university? Did they marry their childhood sweetheart? Were they an only child? They might have had an illness which caused problems whilst they were growing up. Write about anything you think that might have shaped them and brought them to this point.

A word of caution: it is not unknown for a writer to use their own back story. That leads you into the world of autobiography. If this happens to you, be very careful not to get into extremely personal details because you might find it difficult to step back from the narrative and assess whether your characters are developing properly. You will be too close to the incidents you're writing about and your judgement might be impaired.

It is worth mentioning here that novels are normally divided into two categories: those that are plot-led and those that are character-led.

By plot-led, I mean the novels of someone like John Grisham who carefully guides his characters through the plots he has devised for them. Although the characters are an important element of his novels, the plot is the integral part of his books.

Novels by a writer like Anne Tyler are character-led. She starts with an introduction to her characters and then builds a life for them, what they come up against and how they cope.

In the book *The Writer and Her Craft*, Anne Tyler says:

'When I was painting the downstairs, I thought of a novel to write. Really, I just thought of a character; he more or less wandered into my mind, wearing a beard and a broad-brimmed leather hat. I figured that if I sat down and organized this character on paper, a novel would grow up around him.'

That novel became *A Patchwork Planet* and the central character does indeed have a beard and a broad-brimmed leather hat. This is a perfect example of how a character can be the basis for a novel, testing him and finding out what happens around him.

It is fair to say that the characters will develop through the events of a novel. It has been said many times by many writers that 'a character ran away with me. I didn't know they were going to do that'. Writers say that once they put characters into an environment on the page and begin writing chapters, giving the characters dialogue, events to overcome, those characters will have a life on the page. You will find that, as their life progresses, it will be easier and easier to write about them, because not only will you be getting to know them better, you will also be able to recognise what they're capable of and what you can expect of them.

Bring your characters alive by imagining how they feel and think. For me, this is one of the best aspects of writing: the heady feeling, the building up of a character, getting to know their personality, deciding what they're capable of. I can move them around, put them in different scenarios, see how they behave, and how they react to what I've given them.

There is also potential here for an element of surprise. By showing what your character can do, and what they do on a regular basis, you are then able to introduce another dimension by giving your characters a challenge, something that would make them behave in an uncharacteristic fashion. Your character may have been a bachelor all his life, sticking to a rigid timetable, eating at the same time every day. Having established that pattern of behaviour, you can then overturn it by introducing into his life something or someone new. This could throw all his carefully adhered to rules into the air.

Now that you have your character, spend a moment checking that you haven't fallen into any stereotypical traps. Characters can be archetypes, but not stereotypes. Archetypes are universally recognised prototypes or examples of a certain character type. They've been present in literature for centuries and can serve as an acceptable form of 'shorthand' if you're describing a minor character. By contrast, a stereotype is an oversimplification or generalisation of a type, and should be avoided in your main characters. By conforming to stereotypes, your writing loses its edge and your characters could become weak or unmemorable. Do all little girls wear pink? Are single mothers always poor? Is football the only sport for boys? Are all drug addicts homeless?

Archetypes
* The mother-figure
* The star-crossed lovers
* The flawed and brooding hero
* The wise-cracking detective
* The jolly, rotund sidekick
* The mad scientist
* The whore with a heart

Stereotypes
* The friendly vicar
* The shy librarian
* The genial landlord
* The homeless junkie
* The thieving traveler
* The flamboyant homosexual

You should aim for your characters to evolve. By the end of the novel, something inside them must have shifted or altered in some way, maybe for the better, maybe for the worse, but a change will need to have taken place. In reality, we do change, maybe not in a dramatic way but a subtle change will have been wrought in us due to the circumstances we find ourselves in. That should be the same for your characters.

Appearance

Appearance is important in all aspects of writing and particularly so when describing characters. Details that are well-placed give a strong sense of authenticity, helping the reader build a mental picture of your character. So much of this depends on visualisation – on how the reader sees each character. What colour hair has he got? Does he pull an expression when he's talking? Does he use his hands a lot? Are his trousers too short? Does he always wear blue? Is that his favourite colour?

It's not only the outward appearance that's important, it's also the trappings that surround each one of us. For a novelist, this is when details are so important. If your character reads a paper, say which one it is: *The Times*, the *Daily Mail*, *The Sun*. Again, care needs to be taken when writing these details. The stereotypical picture of someone who reads *The Sun* needs to be carefully thought through. Not every *Sun* reader drives a white van, but it's an inescapable fact that by reading a certain paper, our characters will be immediately labelled by readers, so think this through carefully before you decide which paper.

Similar rules apply when choosing a car for your character. What type of car do they drive? A BMW, a Ford, a Rolls-Royce? Choose these carefully, avoiding the trap of putting a pin-striped director in a BMW or a retired High Court judge in a Rolls Royce. By careful use of these details, your reader will be able to place the character and put them into the surroundings that the reader knows and recognises. Bear in mind that no matter how well you think you've described your character, your reader must be able to visualise the scene you've portrayed.

This excerpt from John Steinbeck's novel *Of Mice and Men* is an example of how he portrays his character:

> *A tall man stood in the doorway. He held a crushed Stetson hat under his arm while he combed his long, black, damp hair straight back. Like the others he wore blue jeans and a short denim jacket. When he had finished combing his hair he moved into the room and he moved with a majesty only achieved by royalty and master craftsmen.*

This is beautifully written – we can see this tall man, we've seen enough films about men who work with cattle to enable us to fill in any gaps in the description.

The writers of good fiction recognise that people are extremely complicated and, by creating characters so convincing, we fully expect to see them standing behind us in a supermarket queue. It's not easy to develop characters with this depth and richness. Many writers, who have a sketch of a character in mind when they begin a story, sometimes find that their character cannot make it beyond the initial sketch. Their characters are wooden, a cardboard cut-out. All too often this happens when the original plan for a character is not built upon. If this happens to you, go back to your original notes, delve a bit deeper into the character's personality, build up his background. It is worth remembering that, as a writer, you don't have to explain or even know exactly what's making your characters do what they do; your only obligation is to make their actions convincing to the reader. This relies heavily not only on your instinct or intuition about people, but how well you've drawn your character.

In real life, when meeting someone for the first time, they are unknown to you; it will take a while before you get to know them properly, to find out their traits, their personalities, their strengths and weaknesses. The same is true of fiction; the character's life will evolve during the course of the novel.

One question that I'm repeatedly asked by students is, how can you write about a character who is evil, someone who makes no concessions at all to the rules that most of us live by? Again, the same principle applies, your reader does not necessarily have to like your character, they merely have to believe in them. They may not care for them but you should aim for an empathising, a sympathising with their predicament so you can write about them in a complete way. You should understand what drives your character to do a deed, whether that's murder or the robbing of old ladies. If you cannot warm to your characters, neither will your readers, your antipathy will seep through your writing and it will be picked up by readers. Writing should always make your reader turn the page, wanting to know more, wanting to know what happens next.

This is where your character's back story comes in very useful. You as writer will know that something has caused them to behave in the way they do. And, once again, this is where your initial work on characters comes into play, and why it's essential to do a thorough job on your character sketch. You will have written about the choices he's made and the decisions which have shaped him.

It might be that you don't use the entire back story, it is enough that you know it and you will certainly need to know it so that it informs your writing and character development. Your job is to make certain that these fictional characters behave in a way that will help move the novel along and also seem reasonable to the reader, given what they know about them.

You may have a character who continually lies. Your reader knows the truth and can recognise what makes that particular character lie.

There is scope here to make your characters into complex people. They may even be called 'larger than life'. Not overly so, just enough perhaps to seem a little bit more eccentric than the people you meet on the street. If you analyse some of the characters in your favourite novels, you might find these characters are slightly exaggerated, maybe even a little more impressive than real flesh and blood.

Most readers will tell you that they turn the pages of a novel to find out what happens to the characters – they care about them, they want to know what is happening to them. It is that caring that you should be aiming, for that 'need to know' factor, that curiosity about what will happen next. Bear in mind that there are no bad characters, just bad writing.

Now, what's stopping you from making a start?

■ EXERCISE

Begin with an A4 sheet of paper and list everything you want your character to be. Start with the name, the age, physical descriptions, whether they are working and what they do. Then go on to describe where they live, who with, what breakfast cereal they enjoy, what radio station they listen to, their favourite piece of music...think of all the points discussed in this chapter and see if you can work with the character you have created.

3

Voice and Viewpoint

Voice

One of the things that can bring characters to life is their voice. By that, I mean the way they talk and the way they think. Each one of us uses language differently and even fictional characters have a voice that is unique to them. Although you're writing fiction, you don't have to adopt a special literary way of using language. You can break the rules of grammar and 'good' English if you think it's necessary for the characters and the plot.

When planning your characters' voices you need to think about where they come from. Would they have an accent? Is there a figure of speech which is natural for their environment? For example, true Eastenders often say, 'D'you know what I mean?' at the end of their sentences, rarely stopping for the answer. Would your characters have these sorts of verbal tics? Do they fail to pronounce any letter of the alphabet? It is essential to think about the way your characters talk. This might have been something you've already included in your character sketch, for example your central character might have a strong Irish accent. Your character's speech pattern will be part of them, not only in the dialogue but in the narrative of the novel.

There are no rules with voice – it's more a matter of intuition. Ask yourself "does this voice sound right for my novel?" As you develop the collection of voices that you can employ, you will gain a greater depth and range as a novelist.

Viewpoint

By viewpoint I mean who is going to tell your story? This is an important choice for a writer because it's the viewpoint character who will win over readers and engage them in the story. All stories are told from someone's point of view – so who is telling yours?

Viewpoint is the tool through which your story is told.

If you have a strong central character, the decision might be made for you and you will write your novel from that character's viewpoint without needing to give it much thought. If you're writing a spy thriller, will the spy tell the story? Or will it be someone from the KGB? Or will it perhaps be the spy's mother?

It may be that you're writing from a child's perspective. If so you are immediately limited by the language you can use. It would be wrong for the child character to sound too mature and equally it would be wrong for the character to be too childish, rendering the story incomprehensible.

The key is to find a balance, a halfway point when the

26

language from a child can be understood and appreciated by an older reader.

> **Bestselling crime writer Patricia Cornwell wrote three novels which were all rejected before her agent ventured to suggest that she might have chosen the wrong person as her viewpoint character. It was suggested that she try writing from the viewpoint of one of her minor characters, the forensic pathologist Dr Kay Scarpetta. The result is a publishing sensation, with Scarpetta investigating her nineteenth case in 2009.**

First Person Viewpoint

Writing in first person gives your writing a sense of immediacy; it can have greater dramatic effect than third person. First person is by far the most clear-cut, the 'I' telling the story from your protagonist's point of view. This obviously means too that there can only be one point of view, that of the narrator, the 'I'.

In my novel *Missing Nancy*, I used first person for the character of Jonathan, a 12-year-old boy. Here is his voice in the first person:

> *No-one knows I talk to my dead grandmother. It's not the sort of thing you say to people. She'd always said that she'd keep an eye on me and I prefer that to the way mum says she's watching me.*

The first person viewpoint does have its drawbacks. The reader can only experience events through this narrator's eyes. Information and other events in the novel will have to be reported back to the protagonist, so if your plot is a complicated one, there may well be a great many messages and phone calls within the text so that the reader can be told what the other characters are doing.

Matthew Neale, the author of *English Passengers*, says: "The first person is more limiting. If you have one narrator, which is usually the case, you have to follow them slavishly wherever they go. You can't reveal things your character doesn't know. This can bring problems of structure and you will probably have to work harder to bring variety between scenes to avoid your character running into the same people several times in succession."

A word of caution: when writing first person take care not to write reams about your character's thoughts, views on life and what a wonderful person they are. Would you want to listen to someone doing that? Why subject your readers to it?

Third Person Viewpoint
In first person you have insight into and understanding of the central character, but in third person you have access to the thoughts and emotions of all the other characters. If you choose to work in third person, you will use 'he' or 'she' or 'they'.

It could be argued that third person lacks the familiarity and immediacy of the first person, but writing in third person does offer a writer tremendous scope. All your characters can go wherever they like. You can place them wherever you choose.

In *Missing Nancy*, I alternated Jonathan in the first person with that of a third person viewpoint for his 79 year-old grandfather:

The silence in the garden was broken only by the harsh gulping sound as Frank tried to drink the scaldingly hot tea. He cleared his throat and tried again, 'So, Jonathan, what's this all about then, this trip to France. When was this decided?'

Frank knew he looked ridiculous, his blazer had bunched up around his ears, his trousers had risen up, exposing his skinny legs and his highly polished brown shoes seemed far too formal for sitting in a garden.

Bestselling author Val McDermid says about first or third person viewpoint: "Each style has its advantages and disadvantages. With first person you have a much closer and more intimate relationship with the reader. But you're restricted in what you can show because nothing can happen that the narrator isn't witness or party to. In my novels with Brannigan, there's no possibility of revealing the inner life of the criminal. In other novels, particularly those that involve an ongoing police investigation, it's important to be able to show various strands unraveling at the same time, so it becomes necessary to open up the point of view to embrace more than one character. But I have to work harder at building a relationship between the protagonist and the reader."

Multiple Viewpoints

What do you do if you can't decide whether you have a central character? Perhaps you've written about three or four people, all of whom could tell the story. This can be done – if your characterisation has been well thought out, your readers will be able to identify with each of the characters as they progress through the novel. You might have different chapters of your book told by different characters. Or your story may easily divide into several parts, each narrated by a different character.

Bestselling author Sarah Waters did this in her hugely successful 2002 novel *Fingersmith*. Part One is told by Sue Trinder, an orphan and housemaid who is raised in a den of thieves. In Part Two, the story is taken over by Maud Rivers, before returning to Sue for Part Three – and a breathtaking finale.

It's your decision as a writer to decide which one has centre stage when they are together and which character's movement to follow when they are apart. Novels with multiple viewpoints are tricky even for experienced writers as they can be difficult to follow and difficult to track.

A word of caution: when writing with multiple viewpoints, be careful not to change viewpoint halfway through a scene. An example of this would be:

> *When John watched Mary cross the room, he thought how tired she looked. Mary knew John was watching her, she smiled, she knew she looked tired.*

There are two characters' thoughts in those two sentences and it can be disconcerting to read. Some critics refer to it as 'head-hopping', and it's best avoided in contemporary fiction because it can create a sense of disorientation in the reader.

One way to avoid this would be to keep to one character's views in one chapter and switch the viewpoint to the other character in another chapter. As each new chapter begins, one character tells the story, and in the following chapter, another character takes over, thus enabling viewpoint to be shared. By writing this way, you can easily focus on two or more characters and allow the reader to understand how each one is handling the situations they find in the novel, viewed independently of each other

When I'm writing in the third person I try to focus on one central character, working on their moods and thoughts and understanding of those in the scene with them. In this way, although the other characters take a lesser role, I can still follow their progress and my readers can have access to their thoughts and feelings. An example of this would be:

> *John looked at Mary. He knew what she was thinking, she'd said it many times before – she wanted him to change his job.*

Second Person Viewpoint
It's worth making a brief mention of the second person viewpoint. In second person, the prose speaks to 'you', as in this example:

> *You walk down the corridor, your feet making no sound on the carpet. Your heart is racing.*

Iain Banks uses second person narrative in his book *Complicity*:

> *You hear the car after an hour and a half. During that time, you've been here in the darkness, sitting on the small telephone seat near the front door waiting. You only moved once, after half an hour, when you went back through the kitchen to check on the maid.*

Writing in the second person is unusual and can be demanding. In a big novel, it can take an enormous amount of stamina for a writer to stay focused. It can also a difficult tense to read without feeling unsettled – so to avoid disconcerting your readers I would advise avoiding this viewpoint unless you're keen to experiment or feel very confident about your abilities.

Third Person Omniscient
I should also mention one more viewpoint, that of the third person omniscient narrator. This may sound complicated but

it isn't. It merely means that there is another all-seeing, all-powerful voice telling the story. This technique was used by many 19th century writers, who would often say something along the lines of, 'And now would be a good time to return to Henry, for he's been waiting for a long time, unaware that Mary has spent two hours talking to another man'.

This is the voice of an unseen (but all-seeing) narrator who tells the readers what is happening on the page. I would strongly advise you to avoid the third person omniscient. In modern fiction it's far easier and more interesting to write in either third or first person – unless, of course, your novel is an echo of a 19th century novel.

■ EXERCISE

An anecdote about Salman Rushdie tells how, after having written one of his novels in third person, he then changed his mind and re-wrote the entire book in first person. Writing a novel once is hard work, so writing it twice takes dedication and weeks or months of even harder work. Better to get it right the first time! Try writing a scene using the first person viewpoint. Describe everything that happens from the 'I' position. Play with the words. Interact with other characters and the environment. See what you discover about the possibilities, and the limitations, of this viewpoint. Now re-write the same scene using the third person viewpoint. Gauge which of the two you prefer and which gives you more scope.

4

Dialogue

Conversation
Realistic but not real life
Speech patterns
He said, she said
Trim your adverbs

Learning to write believable dialogue is arguably the hardest skill a writer needs to develop. Important scenes in your novel will rely on dialogue and you need to be able to capture the drama by writing good, clear dialogue.

Remember that dialogue is conversation – conversation between your fictional characters. It should convey information not only about that character but about what's taking place on the page.

To become a novelist, you should be aware that the trick of writing good dialogue is making it seem authentic. That is, not copying real conversation, but imitating it. If we think about the way we speak, our conversations are often rambling and repetitive, lacking in depth or trailing off without coming to any conclusions. This isn't how to write dialogue. Your readers will be bored to tears. You're aiming for believable dialogue, a conversation between your characters, words that flow without superfluous chat. Combined with that, there should be a sense of it being part of your story. Think of dialogue as a device to move the plot along, to convey information.

We see this in soap operas, which rely heavily on their characters giving each other a reminder of what went on in previous episodes:

> *"How did the interview go? The one for the job of manager at the new outlet centre?"*

In real life people don't talk to each other like that. You should steer clear of sounding unreal, long-winded. Dialogue should be used to great effect to express character. Good dialogue can say a lot about your characters: it can express their moods, their aims, and their relationship with other people. This example from Alan Bennett's *The Uncommon Reader* demonstrates:

> *"I gather," said the equerry, "that it might be advisable if Your Majesty were to see Sir Claude in the garden."*
> *"In the garden?"*
> *"Out of doors, ma'am. In the fresh air."*
> *The Queen looked at him, "Do you mean he smells?"*
> *"Apparently he does rather, ma'am."*
> *"Poor thing." She wondered sometimes where they thought she'd been all her life. "No, he must come up here."*
> *Though when the equerry offered to open a window*

she did not demur.

"What does he want to see me about?"

"I've no idea, ma'am."

Sir Claude came in on his two sticks, bowing his head at the door and again when Her Majesty gave him her hand as she motioned him to sit down. Though her smile remained kindly and her manner unchanged, the equerry had not exaggerated.

Good dialogue, as shown in this example, will ensure that your reader will feel connected to the character – even feel sympathy for the Queen!

Speech Patterns

It is important to differentiate between each of your characters' voices so that they each sound different on the page. A titled lord will not have the same speech pattern as that of a painter and decorator, unless they'd both been educated at Eton. Northerners' speech will be different from Southerners'; an 18-year-old girl's will be different to that of an 89-year-old grandfather.

Concentrate on not just the words your characters say but the way they say them. For example, you might be writing about a headmaster who has always spoken in a slow, measured way or a teenager who has an inflection causing her voice to rise at the end of every sentence, as if asking a question. Try to hear the rhythm in your mind as you write.

It is relatively easy to get these verbal quirks across using third person narratives by describing what the other characters think. In the case of the headmaster, you could write at the beginning of the novel that his wife had always hated his slow, pedantic way of talking, thereby establishing his speech pattern (and that his wife loathed it). Similarly, if you're writing about a teenage boy who peppers his sentences with 'like' then use 'like' lightly otherwise the reader's concentration may wander. This will get your point across to the reader without needing to constantly bring it to their attention.

Personally, I'm not a fan of accents or odd patterns of speech being used in novels. I find that this can be irritating to read, as it might mean misspelling words or using the vernacular. If you have a character with a strong accent, I recommend suggesting this subtly when you first introduce your character. You could state at the beginning of your novel that 'John spoke with a strong Welsh accent', and then sprinkle reminders at intervals in the narrative. In this way you avoid the risk of exasperating your reader with unintelligible words. Equally, if your teenage lad, the one who says 'like' often, merely put a few 'like' in his initial sentence, the scene will have been set and it's not necessary to punctuate his dialogue with that word throughout the novel.

If your novel is set in another country, a non-English speaking country, it is relatively simple for the writer to insert an occasional foreign word, preferably one that is likely to be recognised. This acts as a reminder without bogging down the prose with vast chunks of foreign words.

Revealing Character

You can say a lot with dialogue. For example, if your character is a hypochondriac, this can be conveyed not merely by dialogue alone, but the trick here is to show how other people react to his endless complaints about ill health, thus cutting back on a long, rambling discourse. This could work by writing dialogue in the following way:

> *Ernesto began talking again about the pain he could feel in his arm, 'I really think this time it's something serious.'*
> *Maria stifled a yawn.*

By showing the effect Ernesto's words have on Maria, her stifled yawn, we have avoided lengthy dialogue, but your reader knows immediately that Ernesto is a bore about his health. Remember in an earlier section I said that every word your characters utter should demonstrate the sort of people they are. This is, once again, where your initial character notes can be very useful. If you've gone into your characters thoroughly, you will know instinctively how they will speak, what impact their words have on others.

Attributions

These are the words that we use when writing dialogue for example, 'he said' and 'she said'. Some editors and writers refer to them as dialogue tags.

Be aware of banality in the dialogue and search out the irrelevant words. Focus always on moving your plot forward.

Attributions or dialogue tags are very useful because by exercising a word choice you can demonstrate what your characters are feeling when they speak. If there's a full-blown argument, your character might 'shout' or 'yell'.

Each piece of dialogue by each character should be written on a new line:

> *'I don't want to see you any more.' shouted Ernesto.*
> *'Suits me,' said Maria.*

By doing this, you've established a pattern of speech and it will be fairly easy to establish which character is speaking if you decide not to use attributions for a few lines. If you've got a clear difference between your characters, your reader will instinctively know which one is speaking. There are a great many writers who don't use attributions, and you may prefer not to, but to avoid losing the reader in a quick-fire exchange, you might anchor them by using a single attribution halfway through.

I would always recommend using a thesaurus when writing, it's an invaluable tool – but be careful when using it to choose words for your attributions – it would be easy for the reader to become hopelessly confused when faced with complicated or old-fashioned attributions such as 'expostulated'. You might feel that 'he said' is boring and you want to look for something else, but as in so many areas of writing the simple words are often the very best ones to choose. 'He said' and 'she said' are almost invisible and should always be used in preference to 'he snarled' or 'she asserted', which can seem melodramatic.

In your writing, try using pieces of dialogue and separate them from each other by small actions or thoughts. This ensures that the reader knows who's talking. This also has the added bonus of incorporating a non-verbal dimension of a conversation: gestures, body-language, tone of voice and pauses between comments.

> *'I don't want to talk about this now,' Mahmud said. Jane crossed her arms. 'When do you want to talk about it?'*
>
> *'Not today that's for certain,' Mahmud turned to gaze out of the kitchen window.*
>
> *Jane's voice was cold. 'Let me know when you're ready.'*

Adverbs

This is probably a good point to sound a note of caution about adverbs. Adverbs modify verbs and are often words that end with 'ly' – quietly, sharply, wittily, sarcastically. Adverbs are often used to 'tag' dialogue, for example:

> *'Oh, I know all about that!' I replied sardonically.*

> *'They're in the cellar,' Nicky said grimly.*

We were probably all encouraged to use plenty of adverbs in primary school, but experienced writers tend to avoid piling their prose – and in particular their dialogue – with adverbs.

Adding Drama

You can also use dialogue for dramatising an incident, showing the reader the fear or apprehension your characters are feeling. Be aware of the words that are not spoken – the sub-text, the hidden meaning. This can be done by demonstrating your character's body language. If your character is lying, show how he sits, whether he wraps his arms around his body or evades eye contact. These are techniques that can be combined with dialogue to enable your reader to get an instant picture – an understanding of the discomfort, the hidden message, the tensions that are underlying in the dialogue between characters.

Skilfully written dialogue should convey the conversational tone without needing too many adverbs.

Reading your work out loud, listening for the pauses and the emphasis is particularly important for dialogue. Either read it yourself, or ask someone you know and trust to read it aloud for you. Listen to the speech pattern and see where you need to emphasise a word. Listen out for the superfluous words, see where you can tighten up the dialogue to make it more dynamic or listen to see if it needs something extra, a pause to highlight a problem or softer words to soothe an argument. Pauses can be given when writing, by the careful use of commas.

'He looked at her, he knew what she was thinking,' said Nigel.

Whenever you watch a film or a play, you can hear

when the actors are emphasising a point, when their voices lift and fall and you need to demonstrate this in your writing to give your dialogue better effect. An emphasis on a word can be demonstrated by the use of italics (or if the passage is in italic, use plain text for emphasis).

'I didn't say in a minute, I said bring it here now.*'*

When writing dialogue, use exclamation marks very sparingly to avoid running the risk of making your characters seem hysterical. Even more importantly, when you do need to add an exclamation mark, your previous usage weakens it on the occasions when you are trying to make a point.

Often in a dramatic scene in a novel, dialogue is written sparsely. Short sentences carry far more dramatic weight and certainly they have stronger impact. If you have a scene where your characters are in the middle of an argument or a crisis, they would speak almost in a staccato fashion, rattling the words out at great speed.

'Come here now!'
'Go to hell.'
'Do as I say.'
'No! Leave me alone. Get lost.'

It's fairly obvious that these two characters are in some sort of crisis and there is no need to pile on extra words. Under these circumstances, less is definitely more.

If your characters are aggressive and your plot revolves around their aggression, just like the accents, there is no need to work the aggression into every sentence. The focal point is the aggression so all you need to do is give your readers an example of how the character behaves if it is essential to the plot. In all other cases, a recap will be enough to remind your readers.

Finally, if your character studies are thorough and that includes their speech, by the end of the novel, your readers should be able to identify each character by their voice without you spelling it out.

■ EXERCISE

Study the way your favourite writers use attributions and how they set out dialogue on the page. Take a piece of your own dialogue and apply these examples to your own characters. Does it make your writing seem more professional? Can you improve on the way the experts are doing it?

5

Setting

Background
Location
Research
Time Period

Where should you set your novel?
What's the perfect background and location for your plot?
You're the author, so you have complete freedom here.
It's your novel, your choice!

    With the range of modern research tools at your disposal you can choose to set your novel anywhere in the world. However, authenticity is important if you don't want to run the risk of losing well-travelled readers. The Internet is an excellent research tool. Without setting foot in Fiji, you could place your novel in a town close to the sea. You can write about the language, the inhabitants and the customs. Guidebooks are also useful, as are street maps, A-Zs and films set in the place you're using.

    If you're setting your novel closer to home, you can

still use the Internet to seek out the main buildings, the history of the town to use in your writing. One of the most important elements of setting is that your reader must be able to experience it with you.

If you want to set your novel in the town you grew up in or where you're living now, you will have firsthand experience of the streets, the open spaces, what day the market is held on, but even with first hand knowledge, there are things that can be overlooked. I'd strongly recommend, whenever possible, walking around the streets you will be using: check out their names, where the roads intersect, whether there are trees lining the streets, or if there's a children's playground nearby. Listen out for the noise of the traffic, the sound of children playing in the park, all the things that you probably had not been aware of before.

Setting is important. It can be used to control the way your plot moves forward. The environment in which your characters interact can shape the action. The climate can provide colour and mood.

If you're describing a hotel, visit the reception area, take a note of how many chairs there are, the smell of the hotel, the noise the porters make when they wheel suitcases in and out of the doors. As with your character sketches, you may not need all this background information but it will be invaluable when preparing a believable setting, because the information you don't use will still form part of the background – you'll have it in mind when you're describing the setting.

Even if you're writing about a non-existent place, a town that you've made up, detail is still necessary to create an atmosphere of authenticity. Use what you do know, maybe it's an amalgamation with the place you're living in, mixed with other towns and cities, blend the details together, making a cohesive whole. It is important for your reader to believe in even a non-existent town and you will achieve this by using credible detail.

Time Period

Remember that setting is about more than just location. You should consider the time period and how this might affect your characters. Setting your novel in the past might allow things to happen which couldn't happen in the present day, and so create tension and conflict. Equally, setting your novel in the present day allows you to use technology to advance your plot and show your characters communicating in a contemporary way (emails, mobile phones, texting and Twitter!).

■ EXERCISE

Write three paragraphs on a place where you had a memorable holiday. Go into detail: list the sounds that you heard, the landscape, the buildings that you visited. Describe the colour of the stones, the flowers that grew. Search your memory for each detail and then read through what you've written. Have you done justice to this place you're describing? Are there more details you can use?

6

Plotting

Real life
Character- or plot-led
A dilemma
Timing
Twists and turns
Plot types
Subplot
Theme

We've established that most novels are either character-led or plot-led, so in this chapter let's focus on plotting.

It can be daunting to consider plot in detail, but remember that 'plot' is merely another word for what happens to us in real life. We don't have plots in our lives, we are dealt with a series of circumstances, problems or tasks and we learn how to cope, how to handle what life has thrown at us.

The art of good plotting is learning how to manage the events that we have devised for our characters. What you also need is the ability and tools to tell your story so well that readers will turn the pages, trying to find out what happens next.

As a general guide, aim for something to happen in every scene, in every chapter, something that will throw your protagonist off balance. Things might get better or worse but they need to be constantly changing. Again, it doesn't have to be high drama, just a sense that your character has moved from their starting point – they need to stay out of kilter, out of their normal routine.

As a writing tutor, I'm often asked how to get plots. For me, the plot depends on my character. Most of the time, I will have a character in mind before I make a start and then I ask how he would cope with the scenarios that I have devised.

* What would he do now?
* What will happen to him?
* How would he cope with this?

I need to ask these questions to enable me to work on charting my character's behaviour and working out how he'd deal with what I've devised. Plot for me always comes via the characters.

The idea for my novel, *Missing Nancy*, came whilst I was on holiday in France. We were staying in a camp site in the Loire Valley and in the pitch next to ours was a young British mother with two children, a teenage boy and a baby boy of about fourteen months old.

The mum appeared to have arrived in France without any of the trappings for a self-catering holiday. Although they had two tents, they were very simple and she had almost nothing in the way of plates, cups or cutlery, The three of them had to eat their meals sitting in the front seats of her Renault Clio and she seemed unable to do anything to entertain the baby, dumping him regularly into the arms of her teenage son who obviously resented this.

I studied her, watched the way she ignored her teenage son and seemed to spend most of her time listening to the radio in her car. I wondered what had driven her to arrive in another country without the very basics that were needed to care for her children. It suggested to me a flight from something, I couldn't quite believe that a mother would have arrived in another country with so little preparation for the trip, so I began making notes on what might have precipitated that flight from home.

This example illustrates how your plot might grow from knowledge of your characters, so your novel is character-led. Some writers prefer to begin with a plot such as a murder-mystery, a bank fraud or a thwarted romance and then place their characters into that plot and see what happens, how they react. If this sounds like you, then your novel is plot-led.

If you're the kind of writer who likes to find a plot first, then search through newspapers, listen for stories on the news, read the obituary columns and court notices.

I have known students who have had a plot ready for quite some time. In some cases it's a scenario that they've wanted to write about for years. If this is true of you, all you need to do before making a start is check that the various components are still as relevant, as authentic as the time when you first thought about it. Things move on, fashions change, so be careful when approaching a long-held idea for a plot.

If your novel is character-led, then it is important to recognise that, at the end of the novel, your central character has either gained or lost something, is altered in some way by what has happened to them. This need not be something as cataclysmic as the sinking of the *Titanic*. By the end of the novel, there should be a general realisation and an understanding that your characters have changed in some way, that they are not the same people who started the novel. Their fundamental thinking should have shifted, but whether they are better people at the end of the novel is up to you.

One tip that I have used in the past is to think about an arc when building your plot. Begin with the opening of your novel, the first time the reader encounters the character and that character has a problem, a dilemma of some sort – perhaps it's a fear of flying. Carry on with the arc theory and in the middle of that arc your character might stumble upon something which puts that fear to the test, maybe they are forced to take a flight, and you need to dramatise the fear and work out how it manifests itself. The final section of the arc marks the ending of the book where the fear is either vanquished or made worse. Whatever you choose, the central character has moved from the original starting point.

Anne Tyler's Pulitzer Prize-winning *Breathing Lessons* offers an extremely good example of a shift in the character's original understanding of her life and the part she has played in it.

Tyler's novel takes the form of a journey. This is a popular way of plotting – putting your characters in a train, a car, a boat, anything that will physically move them from one place to another. This not only charts their progress as they travel but it can also work on another level, documenting the emotional journey they are taking. At the end of the novel, the central character understands a lot more about her marriage and her role as mother.

During the course of the journey, with unexpected detours into the lives of old friends and grown children, we follow her progress. We read about disappointments; the way children can create storms in a family; the way that a husband and wife behave during a long marriage; the changes wrought in them. And finally we read about the better understanding of each other that the characters come to. What Tyler does so well is to demonstrate that over a period of time things change and yet there is a sense of life carrying on as before. Certainly at the novel's finish, there is a change in the central character. She is more aware of what has gone on in other people's lives.

Sometimes a novel will peak too early and, if the plot reaches its climax too soon, little else of importance can happen in the novel, leading to a sense of disappointment in the reader. Plotting is all about timing – leading your reader through a sequence of twists and turns, and towards the end of the novel, the realisation should come that all avenues have been explored, all significant decisions have been made.

With plot-led novels, focus on the situation you're putting your characters in, testing them, seeing how they cope.

If you began your preparations with a detailed list of what you want to happen in your novel, I'd suggest using that list as a provisional template. This way you can keep abreast of the timing – what happens next, what will happen to the characters as your plot expands.

Plot Types

The use of plot will often define the genre of the novel. Knowledge of genre and the way it is marketed can offer a convenient shorthand to potential readers. For example, crime is often gathered in one location in a bookshop, allowing the reader to locate and browse a collection of plots, genres and authors (old and new) that they already know they like.

Wander around W H Smith or Waterstone's and you will see the tables piled high with bestsellers: romances, courtroom dramas, thrillers and who-dunnits. Most of them are there because of the strong plots and the way that events disentangle in the novel. It's a tried and tested formula, one that works extremely well judging by the number of these books that are sold. You buy one of these novels with the expectation that you'll find a tightly drawn plot and a pattern that you've read and enjoyed many times before.

There are expectations within each particular genre and certain customs in the way a writer will present their plot to their readers. A writer of horror will invariably introduce something disturbing very close to the beginning of the novel. There will then follow a series of macabre events that encourages the reader to turn every page, unable to put the book down before reaching the end. These are commercial novels and it is worth noting that the characters in these novels very rarely make things happen, it's usually outside events that propel the novel forward.

Courtroom plots typically have only one decision to make: guilty or not guilty. The novel concentrates on the drama that unfolds in the court and it's quite normal for these novels to feature a series of flashbacks so that the reader will know what transpired before. By the use of flashbacks, the reader can often see for themselves whodunnit and, in the hands of a skilful writer, there might be an open-ended question that leaves the reader to decide for themselves if the protagonist is guilty. It might be that the verdict says he's innocent but your novel would show that he is the guilty party and your ending could be an image of him leaving the court, a free man.

If you are writing a crime novel, explore alternative endings, try them out for size, see what other ways there are to finish your book.

Many crime writers begin their novels with the discovery of a body then move the narrative forward as the investigation proceeds. Flashbacks are used to ensure the reader understands what led up to the death. Bear in mind that the endings of these novels should never be predictable otherwise tension would be lost.

Fans of John Le Carré will know that his books uncover secrets and investigate mysteries. The sense of expectation is never lessened by the understanding of what to expect in one of his novels, indeed it must be the driving force behind a lot of book purchases.

When arranging your own plot, bear in mind that the simplest way of orchestrating time is to arrange it in reverse chronological order. Perhaps begin your novel with a verdict, and then work backwards so the reader will know how the court reached that verdict. This technique can be extremely effective. The real skill here is to write so powerfully that the novel loses nothing by having its dénouement at the beginning rather than the end.

At the end of the novel, your characters should somehow be changed – not a physical change, although this can happen – but a change in their thought processes, their attitude, and the way they view the world.

At the end of the book, you should always aim for all the loose ends to be tied up and the various subplots to be worked through, arriving at a conclusion which gives your reader a sense of satisfaction. Personally, I'd avoid the clichéd 'they all lived happily ever after' ending. Loose ends should be tied up and all conflict resolved, but perhaps there is self knowledge and understanding for the main character even without a traditionally 'happy' ending. You might however be writing a romance and you do want the characters to live happily ever after, but in general terms you should be aiming for a satisfied reader rather than a disappointed one, one who expected another ending. Try out a few endings, see what you can come up with. None of these tips and hints are cast in stone, there is plenty of room to manoeuvre, plenty of scope for you to choose which ending suits your novel best.

There can be another way to end either plot-led or character-led novels where there has been only marginal tidying up with a hint of another ongoing plot perhaps. The reader is left with a question – what happens next? In these novels, the memory of the characters, the way they handled their lives will remain – should remain – in the mind and most readers reach their own conclusions about what happens after they read the last line.

A skilled writer makes their readers care about the characters, so they can picture them and endlessly wonder what their lives will be like once the book is put down. If you choose this as an option, remember that it is not a way of tailing off your novel because you can't think what to do next!

In an open-ended plot, although something has changed for your character – he did get the job, he was cleared of murder – there is a sense of his life carrying on once the novel is finished. Consider the novels you've read recently. Can you remember any that have an open ending? Did you continue to think about the characters for a long time after you'd put the book down? If so, that's what you should be aiming for. The mark of a good book, for me, is a sense of regret that I've come to the end, a real desire to remain in literary contact with the characters and to share their lives for a while longer.

When thinking of plots for your proposed novel, it's important to recognize that there are rarely any brand new plots. If you think of fairy tales, murder and mystery novels, these plots are all relatively standard: Cinderella loses her mother, battles with ugly stepsisters, finds her prince, loses him, then finds him again and they live happily ever after. Jane Eyre battles with a wicked stepmother, finds her prince, loses him and then reunites with him.

In his book *Seven Basic Plots – Stories And Why We Tell Them*, Christopher Booker establishes seven basic plots and gives examples of where they occur in well known books and films:

Overcoming the monster – defeating some force which threatens, for example most Hollywood movies, *Star Wars*, *James Bond*.

The quest – typically a group set off in search of something and (usually) find it, for example *Watership Down*, *Pilgrim's Progress*.

Journey and return – the main character journeys away from home to somewhere different and finally comes back having experienced something that changes them for the better, as in *The Wizard of Oz*, *Gulliver's Travels*.

Comedy – not necessarily a funny plot but some kind of misunderstanding or ignorance that keeps parties apart. This is resolved towards the end bringing characters back together, for example *Bridget Jones's Diary*, *War and Peace*.

Tragedy – the main character is tempted in some way by vanity, greed etc and becomes increasingly desperate or trapped by their actions until at a climax they usually die. Examples include *Devils' Advocate*, *Hamlet*.

Rebirth – the main character is captured or oppressed and seems to be in a state of living death until it seems all is lost, when miraculously they are freed, for example *Snow White*.

Rags to Riches – the main character begins a pauper, but by a mixture of wit, ingenuity and lucky breaks reaches a more comfortable place, for example *Cinderella*.

What you should recognise is that even though the plots are basic, what's important is the way you approach them – the angle that you take will make your novel different from thousands of others. Whatever genre you're working in, be it crime, horror, romance, it's highly likely that someone else has used the same plot. What you should aim for is an entirely different take, so if you're working on a variation of Cinderella, perhaps tell the story from the perspective of one of the ugly stepsisters. Search for the innovative approach.

Tackle it from a different viewpoint. Make it your own. What agents and publishers are looking for is originality and you must learn to balance that with plausibility, with such good understanding of your characters that there can only be one outcome for them. Having said that, remember that a strong story line is essential. You may feel that your writing is quirky, dark or edgily contemporary and that will be sufficient for your reader, but you cannot rely on those to convince a reader. What does work is a strong story line, a clear motivation.

It's also worth remembering that for a first time novelist, experimental writing will be very hard to publish. Once you have been published, then it might be the time to display your originality but even then it might be difficult.

By reading novels by other writers you can see how their plotting is done, how their characters cope with obstacles in their path and how the book reaches a satisfactory conclusion.

Having said that there can only be one outcome for your characters, it's worth noting that some writers begin their novels with no clear understanding of how the book will end – and I admit that this is the way I write. I give my characters their speech, their lives, their habits before I begin the novel and almost every time I've done this, an idea for a plot will eventually follow. On the rare occasions when this simply does not work, I put that character to one side and put another one in its place. The discarded character can be used in something else. A form of recycling.

One writer who puts mundane events into her characters' lives yet manages to pass the page turning test is Anita Brookner. Her novels centre on the lives of quiet, unassuming characters whose daily routines are unbalanced by something relatively minor and it is the strength of her storytelling that makes the reader keep turning the pages to see what will happen to these mild-mannered, genteel characters.

An excellent example of this is from her Booker Prize winning novel, *Hotel du Lac*.

> *Tea, she thought, I need tea. And then a walk, a very long walk along the lake shore and then a bath and change into my blue dress and, by that time, I shall be ready to make the entrance, always so difficult to negotiate, into the dining room. And then there is all the business of the meal to get through which will take a bit of time and after that, I shall sit around and talk to someone, it hardly matters to whom.*

This example gives a very clear picture of this woman and her state of mind. She's obviously on her own and in the process of planning her evening. She works out a way to unobtrusively approach the dining room so that she won't draw attention to her single status.

As you develop your plot and write your own novel, you may find yourself at an impasse, not sure where to take your characters. You may feel that you're stuck and can't see the way forward. You need to get the writing process kick-started and in this situation I recommend asking two words, 'what if?'

* What if he was having an affair?
* What if he broke his leg?
* What if he lost his job?
* What if his house was burgled?
* What if he was wanted by the police?

Try these out, try asking more 'what if?' questions, thinking about how your character would react.

Subplots

A subplot is a subsidiary storyline which runs parallel to the main story. Normally these subplots can add a dimension to the story, which possibly the main plot lacks. Weaving a second plot through your main story can help you to discover new facets of your characters, together with raising conflict levels and create tension. A subplot can involve minor characters, who perhaps may show some light on why the central character is behaving the way he does. The use of subplots can give the central character substance.

Subplots usually involve minor characters, another story running alongside the central characters' lives. As an example, you might want to consider the lives of your character's parents. This would give resonance to the main character, filling in the blanks of their childhood and it could also work if the parents' lives were complicated, giving a reason if needed, for your character's personality, and a possible explanation for why they do things a certain way. For example, if you're writing about a bank robber, a subplot concerning his parents might go some way to explaining why he robs banks.

If you're writing a crime novel, you might want to consider using a subplot to illustrate the back story of the prosecuting lawyer – his home life, what brought him to the law. Is he fighting his personal battles in the courtroom and away from it?

The subplot should never swamp the main story. If you find that it's taking over from the central plot rein it in. Cut it back as you would with an overgrown branch of a tree. If you feel that it deserves a novel of its own, remove it altogether and keep it for another book. Don't allow yourself to be sidetracked by tantalising possibilities that have nothing to do with the central theme of your novel. You need to be selective, even ruthless, in stripping your novel of superfluous subplots. Question what the subplot brings to your novel. If it adds nothing, or perhaps even detracts from the narrative, prune it.

* The subplot should shed light on aspects of the novel and its central characters
* The subplot should always be relevant to the central theme
* Subplots should slow down the narrative of the central plot, adding tension by taking the reader somewhere else at a vital point of the story
* Subplots should be woven seamlessly into the narrative, adding another ingredient to the novel for the reader to enjoy

Theme

Theme lies at the heart of your novel, and should not be confused with your plot. It's an abstract or philosophical idea about what your novel is 'about'.

If that sounds complicated, then let's take the story of Cinderella. She began by being a servant to her evil stepmother and sisters, but her foot was the only one that fitted the glass slipper so she ended up marrying the Prince. Several different themes emerge from this story: the underdog who triumphed, rags to riches, the triumph of good over evil.

I came up with the following themes. Can you think of others?

* Winner takes all
* You can't keep a good man down
* Crime doesn't pay
* Winning isn't important, it's how you play the game
  and my favourite:
* Hell hath no fury like a woman scorned

It might be that you start your novel with a very clear understanding of your theme, or it may be that as you write, you discover exactly what to say. It is important to look out for what the current trends are in fiction writing and bear in mind that something you're writing now might not appear in print for another two years so recognize what is in vogue and likely to be so for some time. Your theme should be as topical as you can get it.

When you next read a novel, see if you can identify the theme, see if the plot points the way to the central theme. When considering the theme for your own novel, you should be aiming for a unifying idea, a cohesive theme that runs throughout your novel.

An interesting point to remember is that, as with Cinderella, a novel might very well have different themes for each reader. It could be that one reader will say that it's 'good triumphs over evil', someone else might insist that it's 'every dog has his day'. But for these readers, although their interpretation of the central core of the novel might differ, they have identified the one they know – a recognizable theme.

Bestselling author Stephen King: "It seems to me that every book – at least every one worth reading – is about something. Your job during or just after the first draft is to decide what something or somethings, yours is about. Your job in the second draft, one of them anyway, is to make that something even more clear."

In her Booker nominated novel *Unless*, Carol Shields wrote about the temporary loss of a daughter, Norah. There had been no disagreement, no discovery of anything out of the ordinary, to make Norah leave her home. Her mother visits her, she makes no demands, she simply ensures that her daughter is comfortable. Eventually Norah returns to the family home.

The novel ends with the following paragraph:

Day by day Norah is recovering at home, awakening atom by atom and shyly planning her way on a conjectural map. We watch her closely and pretend not to. Right now she is sleeping.

There is a rightness about this ending, a pulling in of strands and a sense of things working out at the end and my understanding of the theme in this novel is 'love will conquer all'. I'm sure somebody else will find another theme.

■ EXERCISE

Think about your novel and ask yourself some questions about your main character.

• How would they cope if they were caught up in a robbery?

• What would happen if they lost their job?

• How would they react if their marriage broke down?

These are only a few suggestions. Ask other questions and see what else you come up with.

7

Detailed Writing

Colour
Character
Additional information
Visual impact

I've mentioned detail in the preceding chapters but now I'd like to focus on it in a chapter of its own. It is essential that attention to detail must seep into all aspects of your writing. Your characters and your settings all need this background detail.

In the chapter on characterisation I explained how important it was to say which paper one of your characters reads, and it is this kind of attention to detail that I will focus on now.

When talking of a character picking up a cup, you need to say what colour cup it is. Having done that, perhaps it's a red cup, now you need to go further, what sort of red? A cherry red, tomato red, or perhaps it's the colour of postboxes. It is this attention to detail that is so important in establishing the authenticity of the fictional world you're creating. It is the overall picture you're aiming for, the visualisation of your characters and the world you've set the novel in. Without these details, the picture will not spring into life.

Details can also tell your reader a lot about the characters. In his novel *The Story of Lucy Gault*, William Trevor lists the contents of a workshop:

> *Mr. Sullivan could see a bench with vices, beneath rows of carpenter's tools – hammers, chisels, planes, mallet, spokeshave, pliers, spirit levels, screwdrivers, wrenches. Two tea-chests were crammed with short pieces of timber of different widths and lengths. Saws and coils of wire, a much used ball of string and a sickle, hung on hooks.*

With this detailed list of tools, the reader gets a very clear picture of the workshop and with it, an understanding of the man who put all those tools there. He's a meticulous man, a hard-working man and in this novel he also proves to be a trustworthy man. There is a correlation here, we are led to believe that the contents of the workshop point to someone who can be trusted. If he takes the tools of his job seriously then it would be safe to assume that he adopts the same attention to other things and, as far as this novel is concerned, he is to be trusted.

Equally, if your setting is a neglected room, the same attention to detail can fill in the gaps that your readers have as they picture the room you're describing. If a room is dirty, show how dirty it is. Describe the cobwebs on the ceiling, the many stains on the carpet, the net curtains which are discoloured because of dirt. You should aim for a gradual build up of detail, the layering of one description on top of another.

Novelists use detail to great effect and, as illuminated

in the William Trevor quote, detail can be used in building up the atmosphere, the hidden message, the underlying story that might be behind the characters' interaction.

An example of this can be found in Kazuo Ishiguro's *The Remains of the Day*. Stevens, the butler, has been given time off and borrows his employer's car to drive to the West Country:

> *What I saw was principally field upon field rolling off into the far distance. The land rose and fell gently and the fields were bordered by hedges and trees. There were dots in some of the distant fields which I assumed to be sheep. To my right, almost on the horizon, I thought I could see the square tower of a church.*

The sweeping landscape, the 'rise and fall' of the land gives the passage a sense of freedom, an escape from the stifling duties that Stevens has undertaken all his working life.

It is this attention to detail that will draw readers into the novel and it's important to remember that they will see the world you've created. I'd recommend that you determine, amongst others, the various brands of coffee, the different breeds of dogs, the tones in colour, the type of flower that your character might hold. What is important to remember is that by giving details, you're offering the reader the opportunity to interpret your story and draw their own conclusions.

In one of my classes, a student who was writing about the break up of a marriage had difficulty with a sentence. He was bothered by the flat tone and wanted to know how to lift it. This was easily remedied by the use of detail.

His original sentence read:

> *Clare sat in the living room, she looked at the clock on the mantelpiece.*

We talked about Clare, whether she was on her own, what she was doing there and what sort of mood she was in. With the addition of detail and by shifting words around, the sentence then read:

> *Alone in the living room, Clare listened to the tick of the large clock, a retirement present for her father. She kept her eyes on the faded dusky blue carpet that had been in the room since she was a little girl.*

We now have a sense of the passing of time and the solitary aspect of the central character.

Good writers can slip details into a sentence to give information without the reader being given a description. An example can be seen in Niall Williams' *Only Say the Word*:

> *'Here, will you give it to him?' Jim reaches in and puts the envelope on her desk and she shakes her styled hair very slowly from side to side and touches her glossed lips together and he feels he is a barbarian, crashing against the gates.*

Niall Williams shows the reader the contrast between the two characters, her 'styled hair and glossed lips' portray sophistication, her body language is languid which in turn makes the character of Jim feel crude, 'a barbarian'.

■ EXERCISE

Choose a scene from your novel and re-write it, adding extra details that will allow readers to clearly visualise the scene and its characters. Help them to sense the atmosphere and to get a little more insight into the world you've created.

8

Descriptive Writing

Show, don't tell
Avoiding cliché
Metaphor and simile
Qualifiers

It is important for every writer to be able to supply vivid elements, vivid descriptions of the events and characters in their novel.

This is particularly true if you're writing a novel with an eccentric plot. Your character might have wings as the central character does in Angela Carter's novel, *Nights at the Circus*. The heroine is utterly believable because of the rich and varied descriptive words used by Carter. This type of writing, the bizarre characters and the outlandish plots comes under the banner of magic realism and the secret of this type of writing is in the name – it is both magic and real.

If your novel is about a character with wings, you could ground your writing with credible details to enable your readers to suspend their disbelief. Your character might suffer from fleas. His feathers could moult. His clothes could be uncomfortable, covering his wings as they do. By using these prosaic details, the central character becomes believable, at least for the duration of the novel. If you're writing about the Jolly Green Giant, describe how difficult it is for him to find shoes that fit. Bring the character into the realm of believability.

Show, Don't Tell

'Showing' allows the reader to experience the story, whereas 'telling' is a dry narrative summary. The playwright Anton Chekhov said, "Don't tell me the moon is shining; show me the glint of light on broken glass..."

'Show, don't tell' is an essential skill for any writer to acquire. It means that when describing something, you should show the scene to allow your reader to form an image in their mind. If you merely tell them, the image can never be as clear or engaging. An example of telling might be:

> *John walked towards the door.*

What does that convey? Can you picture John? Not really, because the sentence does nothing to show John. We have no idea of his age, his mood, whether he can walk easily or if he walks with difficulty.

By using descriptive words, the images become much clearer:

> *John sauntered towards the door.*
> *John inched towards the door.*
> *John limped towards the door.*

A woman wearing stilettos might 'totter towards the door'. A teenager might 'scuff his way towards the door'.

An elderly woman might 'shuffle her way towards the door.'

Alternative verbs immediately bring an image to mind that merely 'walking' towards the door does not.

'Show, don't tell' is an essential technique for a writer to master because it helps readers to build up a picture of characters and settings. It nudges their imagination.

'Show, don't tell' should not only apply to characters, it should be used throughout your novel. Show your reader how filthy a kitchen is – pile the sink with dirty dishes, describe the stains on the floor. If your character is overweight, describe how the buttons strain on his shirt. Show a neglected garden by describing how long the grass is, how the weeds are choking the roses.

You should always aim to show your reader. It is not enough to merely say that a woman is pretty or the room was untidy. These are bland words which convey very little. Search for others and always, always remember that you need to show rather than tell if you want a scene to come alive for your reader.

In Anita Brookner's novel *Hotel du Lac* she describes a room in a hotel:

> *The salon was more agreeable than her own room would have led her to expect, furnished with a deep blue carpet, many round glass tables, comfortably traditional armchairs and a small upright piano at which an elderly man, with a made up bow tie, was playing mild selections from post-war musicals.*

The image of a genteel area, the sight of an elderly man with his 'made up bow tie', is very clear. Most of us have either been to a hotel just like this one or we have seen them on television or in a film and it would be our understanding of rooms such as this that would enable us to fill in the gaps.

It is possible when setting a scene – telling your readers how scruffy a room is or, like the hotel, how comfortable it is – to add further layers as the story progresses. As your character moves, whether from house to office or returning to a flat, further mention of the disorder or luxury can be added, thereby adding another nuance to the story. Your setting, whether an untidy home or an immaculate minimalist one, can often say a lot about your character. A spartan home could be an indicator of a personality trait, just as much as a scruffy one.

Give your reader a sense, an image of what's happening on the page, the smells, the sounds, not just the sight.

Use 'show, don't tell' in all aspects of your writing, whether it's a holiday you're describing, a caravan park, 5-star hotel or a garden shed like the one we encountered in the William Trevor novel.

'Show don't tell' essentials:

- Create a visual image with descriptive language
- Add dialogue so the reader can experience a scene as if they were there
- Use sensory language – convey what your characters can see, hear, smell, feel
- Add detail to bring your writing to life
- Use action and movement to engage and involve you reader an unfolding scene

Cliché

My Collins dictionary describes a cliché as 'a word or a phrase that has lost much of its force through over-exposure, an idea, action or habit that has become trite from overuse'.

Does a chin have to 'chiselled?' Do eyes always

'sparkle?' Will a laugh always be 'tinkling?' These tired words, clichéd words shriek laziness or even worse, boredom.

I cannot emphasise enough the importance of seeking out fresh description, a fully-realised word picture that will stay in your reader's mind long after the novel is finished. If you consider why eyes appear to sparkle, you're highly likely to find a new way of describing them.

Obviously not all descriptive words are clichés. Your job as writer is to search out the very best ones you can find to breathe life to your writing, and offer a new slant on an established theme. This is especially true when using imagery as description. If you're describing someone's complexion, avoid the word 'peach'. This is flat, banal and very tired. Look for something else to convey the smoothness, the softness of skin. And, once again, descriptive words can also add another dimension to your character. If he's thoroughly unpleasant, someone who frowns and rarely smiles, search out words to bolster the image you're aiming for.

As a writer you can use this to great effect, directing your reader's response without boldly telling them what you want them to know. For example, if someone is described as having 'an undersized mouth, a thin moustache no wider than a shoe-string', we might see him as miserly, lacking in humour, someone with very little charisma.

Equally, if someone is described as 'fizzing, hair bouncing around her face like drunken corkscrews', we immediately see this character as ebullient, with zest and energy.

In Niall Williams' novel *Four Letters of Love*, he describes a central character in the following way:

> *He was a thin man, tall and wiry, with bones poking out into his skin. His hair had turned silver when he was twenty four and given him a look of age and severity which was later to deepen.*

The image of 'bones poking out into his skin' is extremely visual and there is not a cliché in sight.

The following extract is from Ian McEwan's novel *Enduring Love*:

> *...yet one more dull stranger in the procession lately filing through their home, a large man in a creased blue linen suit, the coin of baldness on his crown visible from where they stood.*

As readers we can see the thinning hair. The 'coin of baldness' is an extremely good example of choosing a different way to highlight a character's loss of hair.

Metaphor and Simile

Metaphors and similes are figures of speech that express the resemblance of one thing to another.

A simile compares two items directly, using 'like' or 'as', and we can see an example in Eve Merriam's *Willow and Gingko*:

> *The ginkgo's tune is like a chorus.*

A metaphor will compare the same things by saying something actually is the item instead of using 'like' or 'as'. A good example can be seen in Alfred Noyes' *The Highwayman*:

> *The moon was a ghostly galleon tossed upon cloudy seas.*

Metaphor and simile are useful tools for a writer to master, and offer another way for you to bring images to your reader's mind. The trick is to keep things simple. An over-complicated comparison will draw the reader's attention away from the story.

In her Booker Prize nominated novel *The Clothes on Their Backs*, Linda Grant writes:

> *There is a picture of them turning the key in the front door, their smiles like wooden postboxes.*

This is a perfect example of a simile. The image is instant and one that readers will immediately recognise.

Metaphor differs from simile in the sense that metaphors are words or phrases applied to an object or action that they do not literally denote, in order to imply a resemblance. I have used metaphor in my second novel, *Glad Rags*, where I wrote about a large, elderly woman trying on clothes:

> *Margaret held her hand out to Mabel. 'Ladies, do you want to try it on?' For a second she pictured the fine, woollen dress stretched across Mabel's vast bosom which usually resembled the shape of a wet sandbag.*

I think the image worked.

As with all aspects of writing, the concept of less is more is especially true when using descriptive words, metaphors and similes. Great care should be taken when describing, because there can be a danger of over-egging. If that happens, instead of the writing flowing, your readers will find themselves pushing up against an overly complicated phrase. You're aiming for an immediate recognition – using a metaphor that your readers will know and can identify with.

Qualifiers

Qualifiers are words that slightly alter the meaning of others, words such as 'often', 'very', 'almost'. These words rarely add anything to the narrative and, in fact, can weaken your novel.

When you read through your work (and we'll be talking about the editing process further on in the book), cut out these unnecessary words, unless by doing so you run the risk of fundamentally changing the meaning of the sentence.

Whilst we are discussing unnecessary words, it seems a good place to also mention getting rid of superfluous adjectives. I had a student who constantly littered his work with words such as **happy** laughter, **gentle** caress, an **affirming** nod. Not one of the words in bold is needed. Laughter is happy, a nod is an affirming gesture, a caress is gentle.

I think my favourite example is one I came across a few years ago. I had a student who firmly believed that he needed to fill his work with very many words in the belief that his readers wouldn't understand what he'd written. With this in mind he wrote about a character who 'shrugged his shoulders'.

I gently pointed out that there is nothing else to shrug. Eyes, arms, legs, feet, the only part of our bodies that are shruggable are shoulders. So 'he shrugged' is enough and I think carries greater weight.

Many novice writers feel the need to fill their narrative with qualifiers, unnecessary adjectives and adverbs. This is probably due to lack of confidence – a fear that the reader will not understand what is being told; a need to emphasise various incidents; an instinct to load the narrative with heavy references and instructions.

Confidence can only be gained by more writing. When undergoing an apprenticeship in any trade – whether it be an electrician, a plumber, a car mechanic – you learn by doing more. The more you write, the more your confidence will grow.

And of course, remember to read, read, read. Study the choices established writers make, and learn from them as you serve your apprenticeship!

■ EXERCISE

In the following five sentences I've used flat, boring words:

June looked at the window.

David turned his head, it was raining.

Chris decided to walk to work.

Aisha didn't want to go out.

Hannah was late in getting to school.

Try re-writing them. Build paragraphs for each, using the techniques learned in this chapter. Remember to 'Show, don't tell'. Convey the same meaning, but with a better choice of verbs. Build a visual picture. Play with words. Use sensory language. Add dialogue. See how your descriptive writing can bring to life your character or setting.

9

Style

Your own style
The author's voice

Writing is a highly personal occupation – we bring so much of ourselves to our prose and it is this naturalness that we should strive for when we write.

You must find your own style; not a copy of someone else's, but your own. This is often referred to as the author's 'voice', which shouldn't be confused with the character's voice or anything to do with first or third person. The author's voice is purely the writer's style, the way they write; the way that you will write.

Voice or style combines many things including syntax, dialogue, figures of speech and imagery, punctuation and especially word choice. It is how you arrange these things that will determine your particular style.

When I urge students to read as much as they can, very often their response will be that they are concerned that they might subconsciously copy the author's style. There is a huge difference between being influenced by and direct copying. All of us absorb what we read. We look at the way the characters are portrayed, the way the dialogue has been handled and we probably do, subconsciously, take parts of someone else's style. It's unlikely that you would copy another author – and if it did happen, your writing would probably be jerky and unnatural. To reassure students who are worried about copying, I sometimes set an exercise where they write in the style of John Steinbeck or Jane Austen. This always ends with students telling me that it felt awkward or contrived.

You may have to write a lot before you realise that you've found your own style; it might be that you need to make a number of starts before you understand what your style is. Your style will be unique to you, and as individual as the way you speak.

I hope it does come easily for you, but if you feel unhappy with the way you've started on your novel, I would suggest trying it again, loosening up with the dialogue, altering some of the narrative and see if you're more comfortable with that. Try to relax and not force the pace. As your confidence as a writer grows, your style will evolve. You'll know when you've found it!

And in the future it will be apparent to your readers, too – it will be easily identified with you and each book you write.

■ EXERCISE

Re-read some of your favourite authors and try to identify what gives them their unique style and author 'voice'. Is it the length of their sentences? Their colloquialisms? The way they handle dialogue? The humour in their writing?

10

The Passage of Time

Moving things along
Maintaining the pace
Flashback techniques
Tense and the past participle

Writing about the passage of time can cause problems for a new writer. Unless your novel takes place over a week, you will have vast chunks of time when nothing much happens. If you're writing about a family, your characters will need to be grounded – that is, they will have to do the domestic chores, the washing, the shopping. However, reading about these domestic details is not only boring, it also slows down the pace of the novel.

A simple way of moving things along is just to use words which simply but effectively convey that time has passed: 'Two days later..' Your reader's imagination will fill in the blank days and you can proceed with the narrative.

One author who uses words with great skills and to great effect in this way is Arthur Golden. In *Memoirs of a*

Geisha he weaves mention of time passing into the story telling. For example:

During the rest of the spring and that summer...

One morning quite some months later...

For a week or two after Granny died…

Another way of demonstrating that time has passed is the way you present your work. A double line space between paragraphs in your manuscript is a literary convention which lets the reader know that a period of time has elapsed.

By using these suggestions to convey that time has passed, it's worth noting that maybe one of your chapters concerns the events of one day, whilst another chapter might take place over a month and if this is true of your novel, my experience is that readers accept this without question. They are, we all are, used to the inconsistent sequences of time.

It is important to recognise what events are key to your story and these events should be told with great care, slowing the narrative down. Then, when nothing much happens, the tempo increases. Be decisive – if you've written a long, rambling piece about the way your character washes the floor, ask yourself if it adds anything to the story and if not, delete it. You can mark that the kitchen floor has been washed by simply writing, 'She'd completed all her chores...' There is a sense of time passing. A simple statement of this sort is enough.

Flashback
Flashback is a method often used in films when the actors' previous lives are shown as an earlier event before their current situation appears on the screen.

Flashbacks are an easy tool to use. You write as if you were writing a normal scene – the difference is that the action happened before the main events of your story. Readers will know immediately that the scene is from an earlier time in the characters' lives because the use of flashback is a common literary convention. As mentioned in the previous section, the use of double line spacing or the start of a new chapter will indicate that the time has shifted.

A note here on the careful use of tenses. Within a chapter, the tense should remain the same unless you're using flashbacks. When you go back in time, use the past participle 'had' to indicate to the reader that they are entering a flashback. For example:

He had walked to the shop that day.

This denotes a passage of time, and carries more substance than the use of 'he walked to the shop,' which signifies something happening in the present or recent present.

Previously, I have mentioned how a writer can inform readers something about a character by describing the effect they have on those around them. As a way of telling your readers about something that happened in the past, a similar process can be used to convey information about something that had happened earlier. An example of this would be the following extract from my novel, *Missing Nancy*:

> *Frank's parents had died within three months of each other, his father dying first and Frank had always felt that his mother enjoyed her widowhood. He'd find her in the kitchen, wrapping her arms around her chest as if she was giving herself a congratulatory hug on having the good sense not to die first, as if she'd finally outsmarted her husband.*

There is another way of looking back and that is by using your character's thoughts. Your character might be remembering, like Frank, an event in their childhood, it might be something that has had an effect upon them and it is a simple matter to inform your readers of their earlier life.

When using your character's thoughts, showing them remembering earlier events, it is enough to say:

> *John thought of the day he'd been fired, the sadness that he felt when he cleared his desk, the fear he had when he tried to think of way to tell his wife that he'd lost his job.*

Background information is passed on to the reader and it's an easy way of letting your readers know your character's previous history and what has led them to the situation they are in now.

Another tried and tested flashback method is the use of a diary, where the writer can insert the thoughts and plans of a character. However, although this as a method is very well-used, my advice would be to use this only as a last resort because sometimes it can feel like the literary equivalent of a character in a film ripping the days of the week from a calendar. I firmly believe that the thoughts and plans of a character can by conveyed more effectively by the use of dialogue, thoughts and actions. Try and find another, more original, way to describe your character's thoughts, his moods and feelings:

> *He wanted to leave, he'd been planning his escape for a long time. He thought he could go on a Friday, the one day when he was unsupervised.*

At the beginning of this book I spoke about the use

of notebooks and how a writer should carry one at all times. It's worth mentioning here, that for the techniques that have been discussed so far, writing down your thoughts as you try to create flashbacks or begin dialogue, might help you. Trying out various methods before you commit them to your novel can be extremely helpful. Seeing what you have written as you practise, knowing that it is only a rough draft, is often extremely illuminating.

I would recommend trying out the various flashback techniques, see what you can come up with. Once again, remember that there is no rule that says you have to show anyone else what you're trying to do. There's nothing to say that your early attempts have to be aired – it is your notebook, your writing, keep it that way if you'd prefer until you have something that you think is worthy of showing to other people.

■ EXERCISE

Try writing about something that has happened to a character in his childhood. Think about the process involved, the flashback techniques we've talked about. Put your character as an adult in the present, and describe his childhood, and show how an aspect of his youth has a bearing on the person he is now.

11

Stamina

Energy and determination
Procrastination
Tips and techniques to kick-start your writing
Writer's block
Dealing with isolation

Having reached this part of the book, let's assume that you are now writing your novel. You're enjoying yourself. You're writing everyday. And you've got strategies to combat any sense of isolation. Now is the time to consider the stamina required to complete the task.

A novel can be between 60,000 and 200,000 words. To be able to write that amount, to sustain the pace of a novel, requires tremendous energy and determination. Most new writers begin in an excited, positive frame of mind. Invariably this is something they've wanted to do for a long time – it's been thought about, talked about, agonised over, and when the actual writing process begins, it's a heady, exhilarating feeling. That feeling rarely, if ever, lasts for the length of the novel.

I began this book by advising that you should write for a certain period every day and, if you've taken that on board, your daily writing habit should by now be firmly entrenched. You'll need to draw on that habit when the writing becomes slow, your characters seem ponderous and you're feeling drained by the whole experience.

Sometimes when that happens, you only need to leave it alone for a few days, keeping the characters in your mind, before things fall back into place and you return with a refreshed mind and increased energy.

However, there will be times when a short break doesn't work and your despondency is drowning the creative part of your brain. Don't be tempted to make your short break into a longer one. Leaving your work for too long can have a counterproductive effect. The longer you leave it, the harder it is to get back into the writing mood. For many writers, procrastination becomes an art: we sit and stare out of the windows, we wander into the kitchen to make yet another cup of coffee, we check our emails obsessively or find tasks that are suddenly essential to our wellbeing. My favourite is cleaning out the cutlery drawer. Often we will do anything to prevent ourselves from sitting at our desks and writing.

It might be the time to use the tactic mentioned during the chapter about plotting to kickstart the whole process. Ask yourself 'What if...?' Take a sheet of paper and scribble out some ideas in response to your 'What if?' questions. This way you're still writing, still putting words onto the page.

The inescapable fact is that only *you* can get your novel written. The only way to write a novel is by actually writing it – no-one else will do it for you. Remember that there are far more people who want to write than have actually written a novel. You've made a start so you've already done more than many 'wannabe' writers. Give yourself a pat on the back!

If you're still finding it difficult to get back on track,

there are a few techniques that sometimes work for me:

- **Write a set number of words every day**

If you've been writing as I suggested at the beginning of the book, you will be able to tell yourself that every day you'll write 1,000 words. I know of more than one writer who is able to stick to this. If you feel 500 words is more attainable, then write 500 words – find something that will suit you. If, on some days, you are able to write more than 500 words, congratulate yourself, you've passed your target, and then see if you can do it on the following day.

- **Leave a sentence unfinished**

When you've finished for the day, leave a sentence unfinished so the following day, when you go back to your novel, you're caught up immediately in what is happening on the page.

- **Re-read an earlier chapter**

By this I mean reading work you've already done – not editing it, merely reading through. By doing this you can get a sense of the next stage in the writing of the novel, and it should inspire you.

- **Timing yourself**

Allocate yourself a set amount of time in which to write. Put your watch on the desk and write for an hour. If, at the end of the hour, you've got more to write, give yourself another hour and carry on in this fashion.

- **Don't edit – yet**

During the MPhil in Writing that I undertook at the University of Glamorgan, my tutor advised me to keep writing, keep going until I got to the end of my story or novel. The temptation to begin editing your earlier work is very hard to ignore but ignore it you must, because editing can hamper you from every reaching the end. If reading through a paragraph you find an inconsistency or that the dialogue doesn't ring true, make a note of it so you can find it easily later on, but keep writing, keep the words flowing. Editing comes later.

Writing can be an incredibly lonely activity and sometimes a writer can wonder why on earth they're putting themselves through it. Others say they have no choice – they have to write. For me, I'm not comfortable if I'm not writing. I feel something is missing in my life. It can be a hard slog. Working away on your own is often very tough. But when you have finished – when you've finally written THE END – the euphoria cannot be bettered. The sense of achievement is like no other.

I like the anecdote about Alan Bennett who, years ago, phoned Russell Harty and asked him what he was doing. In reply Russell Harty said he was staring at the wall. Alan Bennett laughed and said he was doing the same. So you see, you're in very good company!

There's a saying that goes, "Don't get it right – get it written!" This is a useful maxim – follow your inspiration and get to the end of the novel, then go back and get it right by editing.

Writer's Block

No book on novel writing would be complete without a section on writer's block so I will try to address this condition and to tell you my thoughts and strategies. I must first of all admit that I'm not entirely sure that I believe in writer's block. What I do believe in is lack of confidence, boredom with the whole process, a failure to plan the characters' appearances and the movement of the plot. All of these can be overcome but they require perseverance and energy.

The previous section dealt with stamina, ways of overcoming inertia and strategies to allow you to keep on writing and I believe those strategies can be equally applied to a case of writer's block.

I have had a number of students over the years who have begun their writing in a feverish air of excitement, caught up in the romance, the drama of writing a novel and at roughly the halfway mark their energy had dissipated, their enthusiasm quelled and they tell me that they've lost heart or interest in the project. I suspect for these writers, it was not so much writer's block but an unrealistic view of what writing a novel means.

If it happens to you, you will be swamped with feelings of despair, your self-belief will have taken a knock and you will regret ever telling anyone that it has been your ambition to write a novel.

If your 'block', for want of a better word, is due to a lack of careful plotting, you may need to do some further research to push your story along. It might be that you do not know where to take your character next. This can be overcome by digging deeper into your character's psyche, getting to know them better.

Sometimes, when you've tried just about everything and it still won't work, you can't find the energy and commitment and you wonder why you ever started on this project, then the best thing is simply to walk away from it. Not with the intention of giving it up; but with the view of getting some breathing space between you and your novel. It might simply be that you're tired and need to recharge your batteries. Go out for a walk, take the dog out, mow the lawn but as you do these tasks, keep your novel in mind, mull over the problem that you have.

You may find that breathing space is exactly what you need so that you can return to your novel in a far more positive frame of mind.

Try the tips and techniques on the previous pages, re-read your notes, try to understand what drew you to embark on this in the first place. It is not easy, it does require an enormous amount of courage and determination, but the only one who can write your novel is you.

Isolation

So, you've started your novel, you're writing regularly every day, your character sketches and your ten or twenty point plan are on the table next to you as you write. You've beaten procrastination and writer's block. So far so good.

But what you're might be struggling with, what you hadn't allowed for, is the extreme loneliness of the writer.

Writing is a solitary process. You might be lucky and know someone who is also writing. You might be able to ring them up and say, "How many words did you write today…?"

I would guess, though, that most people write in solitude and have no-one else to compare notes with.

There are many writing groups and courses available that can help in a big way to overcome the loneliness that can overtake us when writing. To be among like-minded people, to be able to share the problems, to give and to receive informed feedback, to support and offer suggestions is incredibly helpful.

If you don't know where to look for writing groups, try the libraries – they should have a list of local groups and local authority adult education courses will have their courses published in their prospectus. Universities often run creative writing courses with the focus on novel writing.

You might have to road test a few groups or courses to see if you could fit in with other members, to see what the group has to offer. My own view is that if a group is running successfully, a new writer can find as much support from the other members as from the tutor. Remember though, that it is your novel and you should be aware of that when listening to feedback. You know how you want your novel to progress and,

Sharing your experiences as a writer as well as giving and receiving feedback on work in progress can help ease the feeling of isolation.

whilst comments from other new writers can be very helpful and positive, you have to write in your own way.

If you're unable to locate or attend a local writing group, you could try joining a distance learning course or online writing groups. I have no experience of these but my personal view is that by virtue of the fact that your work is submitted to an unseen tutor, you're not really reducing your physical isolation as a writer.

Another option might be to attend at one of the many residential writing courses which take place over a weekend, a week, or maybe three or four days. These are often run by published writers who share their own experiences of writing and being published. You may find this stimulating and encouraging and that your enjoyment and enthusiasm will carry you through when you return home.

Final words on writing classes come from Stephen King, who says: "You learn best by reading a lot and writing a lot, and the most valuable lessons of all are the ones you teach yourself. These lessons almost always occur with the study door closed. Writing-class discussions can often be intellectually stimulating and great fun, but they also often stray far afield from the actual nuts-and-bolts business of writing."

12

Research

Libraries
Internet
Personal research

Research isn't always necessary in novel writing. You may not need to do any research at all. It may be that your novel concerns something that happened to your family, or you might want to write about the job you've held for thirty years and your understanding of the subject can't be bettered. However, if you're writing about an event that took place years ago, research will be needed to get accurate information into your book.

In the chapter on setting, I mentioned using the Internet to check up on places and, of course, the Internet may well be your first port of call when digging around for information too. Certainly if your novel is an historical one, you will need a lot of background information on the people and places you want to write about.

The Internet is an invaluable tool, but it would be an appropriate place here to give a word of caution when using the various search engines. Always check who is behind the website and whether they have a biased agenda, or allow anyone to add or edit material. Use reputable online encyclopedias or material published by high quality sources such as universities or the BBC. Be sceptical and check sources and citations.

The library is another place for research, certainly more time consuming than the Internet but you are almost guaranteed to find something that you can use amongst the vast number of books on the shelves.

The other places to try would be museums, other specialist institutions where you can probably find all the information you might need.

I would also strongly advise adopting a proactive line when doing research. I have been working on a novel about a baby who was adopted in the 1960s and by trawling through various websites, I came across an adoption organisation based in Cardiff, where my novel is centred. I sent an extremely polite email asking for help and in a day or two a reply came winging its way back with names of people who would be willing to help me. The information that they gave me was not only extremely helpful, it added another dimension to one of the characters.

Equally, if you know someone in your neighbourhood or from a local school who might be able to help, ask them. I've yet to meet someone who has refused to give information – most people are very happy to talk and share their knowledge.

Bear in mind that your research should be a guideline for you, an accurate one but it leaves you free to play about with some of the facts that you discover. What is important that your reader believes you when you write about facts that they trust you. It may be that the truth you unearth does not fit in with your plot or your characters. If that's the case, leave it out.

Some writers prefer to do their research at the start of the novel; they would be from the first category of writers mentioned at the beginning of this book – those meticulous writers who arm themselves with all the information they need. Others do it as they go along.

I prefer to do some general research before I start and then seek out more information when I get to that particular section. By doing this I've found I tend to get less sidetracked and can remain focused on what I'm searching for.

A word of caution: it is all too easy to lose yourself when researching. One piece of information leads to another and before you know it two or three hours have gone flying by and you've not written a word of your novel.

Research can be fundamental whenever you're writing about something beyond your experience. You can use what you discover to embellish your writing, to pad out the bones of your novel, blending fact with fiction – but at all times striving to make it believable.

13

Editing

Re-reading
The whole picture
Reading aloud
Areas that need work
Second draft

A whole book could be written on the subject of editing. Here I'm going to give you an overview of the editing process and an insight into the tools you need.

First of all congratulate yourself. You've finished your novel. That's the good news. The bad news is that now you start another process and that's editing. Before you start on this task, I would suggest that you leave the novel alone for a few days, a week maybe. Allow some breathing space between you and your manuscript. Look on it as a well-deserved break.

Get An Overview
When you feel ready to go back to work, I'd recommend reading your novel from start to finish. Don't try editing just

yet, simply get a feel of the novel, a sense of whether it works, if it's coherent, whether the characters come alive and whether the dialogue flows.

You might feel very low after the first reading, disappointed by what you've written. You might have embarked on writing a novel with a very fixed view of the book you wanted to write, and here you are at the end feeling that it's poor and not what you intended to write at all. It might help you to know that almost everyone feels like that. Remember that what you're reading is a first draft, not the finished product.

Identify Areas That Require Work

Once you've read your novel through from start to finish, read it again and this time begin to make notes about where you think improvements could be made. Are there places when the narrative slows down? Where the interaction between the characters is aimless and does nothing to drive the plot forward? Be honest with yourself. And be ruthless. Never think a reader won't notice these things – they will.

Underline where you think alterations should be made, and perhaps use a marker to highlight the places where you feel your writing is good. Be prepared to get rid of phrases that stick out like a sore thumb, even those you are proud of. Learn to know what should be kept in and what should be thrown out. You might find that there are whole paragraphs that need re-working. If that's the case, give yourself time to do just that. It doesn't make the novel bad – it's all part of the learning process. You might feel swamped by what needs doing and this is quite normal. Simply allow yourself more time, editing cannot be done overnight.

Look at the way your plot moves, is there enough to keep the reader turning the pages? Can the pace be improved upon? Is there too much description and not enough action? Does enough happen?

Look again at your characters, are they all necessary? Do they each bring something to the novel? Are you asking one character to carry too much of the weight of the novel, would it better if you split the burden between two characters? Who is telling your story? Are they telling the truth? How much do they know? Are the main characters well rounded? Are they stereotyped? What has happened to the central character, has he changed during the novel? Do you show or are you telling? Are all your characters likeable or are they all unpleasant? Perhaps you need to introduce greater variety, demonstrating the good and bad points of each character. Perhaps the novel would be improved if you amalgamated two characters into one. Should your novel be focused on one character, or might it work if you brought other characters in to share the limelight? These potentially are very big changes to make and you need to focus on what works best for your novel.

I've already mentioned the benefits of reading your work aloud while writing, now this same technique will help you in the editing process. Listen to the rise and fall of speech, check that you've not used the same word twice or even three times in one paragraph. Is there a word that you use constantly? Most of us have favourite words we use a lot. This should be avoided. Search for an alternative.

Second draft

It's not unknown for editing to take as long as writing. There may well be two, three, four re-drafts that you need to do. No doubt you will feel overwhelmed by the size of the project, by the many words that need going over, by the checking through of the dialogue. But you've got this far. You've finished a novel. These final hurdles can be overcome.

Keep a very careful eye on the time sequences in the novel. If you've used flashbacks, check the dates and make sure they're correct. Do events run in proper sequence? You might need to rearrange scenes or even an entire chapter. If you find that your time sequences are blurred, be prepared to re-write an entire section again. If it's not clear to you, the writer, then it won't be clear to your readers.

Check the dialogue – can it be improved? Does the novel need more or less? Would breaking speech into smaller chunks give your characters greater impact? Does it create more drama? Are your speakers too long-winded? Does what they have to say sound right? Does the dialogue flow, or does it slow the pace of the novel? Ask yourself, honestly, does the dialogue sound realistic? Does it suit your characters?

Be ruthless
Be realistic
Be questioning
Be brave
Be heard
Be flexible
Be prepared
Be aware
Be descriptive

Do the descriptions work? Is there something else that needs to be described, something that might be enhanced by the right way of describing it? Do they reveal something about the narrator? Go through your descriptions, see where you might add the sense of smell, sound or taste to your work. By adding more description, you could be bringing another facet to your novel.

Check grammar and punctuation

Many writers think that it will be their editor's job to correct their grammar and punctuation. Don't make this mistake. As a new writer your aim should be to submit a manuscript that's as good as it can be. The bar is set high for writers nowadays, and competition to be noticed by agents and publishers is fierce. Editing and correcting manuscripts takes time and costs money. With so many equally good manuscripts landing on their desk each day, an agent or publisher is naturally more likely to choose the one that needs the least work. Don't give them any reason to reject yours – invest in a guide to grammar and punctuation, or research the basic rules online using a reputable site. Check over the tenses in your manuscript. Have you used them properly? Are they consistent? Look at the way you've used commas, are there too many? A wrongly placed comma can change the meaning of a sentence, so be careful. When addressing someone by their name or title, put a comma before the name:

'What do you think, Peter?'

Check that you've correctly used apostrophes. Have you put in too many exclamation marks? Have you used italics properly? Identify clichés and weed them out.

If you're unsure about the grammar, maybe now is the right time to let a trusted friend read the manuscript because someone else's eyes can often spot things that writers have overlooked. There can be no excuses for misspelled words – there is a dictionary and spell-check on every PC.

You might also check for any alliteration that occurs. By alliteration I mean the repeated use of one letter, 'Peter picked up the paper…' in this case the letter 'P'. Once this is read out loud, the alliteration is obvious and can sound comic where no humour was intended. This is the sort of writing that appeals to very young children so if that's your target audience, fine. If not, amend it. A student of mine had written an extremely competent short story but there were five examples of alliteration in a 3,000 word story. 'Her hand hovered over the handle', was one of them and with a few adjustments, we changed the sentence to read: 'She raised her hand and, for a second it remained still, then she gripped the handle'.

By the time you feel you've done enough work on editing your novel, you probably have – to go over it one more time is not only tiring, it's counter-productive. You need to have a sense of when the time has come to leave it alone.

14

Presentation

Professionalism
Fonts
Dialogue
Title
Contact details

When preparing your work, you should aim to get the manuscript looking as professional as possible. Even if you've got no intention of anyone outside your family seeing it, your manuscript should look first rate. You've worked hard, and, when you hold your finished manuscript, you should feel a sense of pride and achievement.

Format your manuscript in 12 point type in a fairly standard serif font. Serif fonts have the little horizontal or oblique strokes at the ends of each character. These strokes make paragraphs of prose in a serif font such as Times New Roman easier to read than a sans-serif font such as Arial. Use double line spacing and type on only one side of the paper. Number your pages and allow generous margins on either side.

Each time a character speaks, indent and give them a fresh line. When the person they're talking to speaks, indent again and give them a new line – that way there will be no confusion about which one is speaking. Earlier in the book I suggested leaving a space to denote that time has passed. This should be a double line space (i.e. two returns). Again, check novels on your bookshelves at home and see how established writers do this, see how they approach dialogue, how they show a lapse in time and decide whether you think it will work for you.

There are various thoughts and suggestions on how to use quotation marks, there are a lot of novelists who don't use them at all. My thinking is that, as a first time novelist, you would be better to use single quotation marks to denote speech and also for quoted words within the text. Double quotation marks when they fall into another pair.

An example of this would be:

'He said I was useless,' said Jamila, 'and he called me a "misery guts".'

In his novel *The Crossing*, Cormac McCarthy doesn't use quotation marks for any of the dialogue between his characters:

Go on to the house and get your supper, his father said.
I'm all right.
Go on, I'll put the horses up.

Again, and this is only my opinion, for a first time novelist, I'd recommend using quotation marks. The more you write, the second novel maybe, you will realize that your confidence has grown and you can do without quotation marks without losing any of the sense of the plot or characters. To reiterate an earlier point, if your characters have been drawn correctly, it will be obvious to your reader which of the characters is speaking because their voice will be unique to them.

Have you chosen a title for your novel? Sometimes a title won't arrive until you've finished the novel, and sometimes you will have had an idea even before you began writing. If there is no title on the horizon, don't agonise over it. It will come. There will be a phrase, or something one of the characters has said, and that will be all the inspiration you need. However, if the title still evades you when you've written, edited, polished your presentation think about your characters, your central theme, your setting. Consider the dénouement. Try playing with the words you've used. Test them for their weight and their meaning. It might be that the central character's name is sufficient (*Billy Liar*). It might be that you find the words that cover the theme of the book (*The Cruel Sea*). You might find that something will pop into your mind when you're least expecting it. I found the title for my novel *Missing Nancy* from an Anne Tyler novel – a character says of his long-dead wife that he misses her 'like I miss water'. I liked the sentiment.

You could always choose a working title until the right one comes to you. It might be that the agent or publisher may have their own idea for a title.

Once you have your title, working or otherwise, prepare a front page for your manuscript and on that page put your name, address, email address and telephone numbers, along with the title of your novel and the word count.

Front Page
- Name
- Address
- Email address if applicable
- Telephone number
- Title
- Word count

Now that your novel is complete, you'll need to decide what you want to do with it. Your manuscript represents a lot of work, many hours of writing, agonising and soul searching. Perhaps you don't want to get it published, you've written it purely for your own sake – so well done on your achievement.

If, however, you would like to see if you can attract the attention of an agent and try for publication, there are more pieces of writing you need to do before you send your manuscript out into the big, wide world.

15

Trying For Publication

Synopsis
Character Biographies
Covering letter
Agent or Publisher
What happens to your manuscript?
Self publishing

Although this book has focused on how to write your novel, my job is not entirely finished if it is your intention to approach an agent or publisher with a view to getting your novel published.

Before you begin the process, it would be worth while investing in either *The Writer's Handbook* or *The Writers' and Artists' Yearbook*. Both of these are published every year and I usually alternate, buying one of the books each year. They are invaluable tools for searching for agents and publishers.

They also carry details of novel writing competitions, short story competitions and give comprehensive information on a number of outlets for writers of fiction. You can study the entries, get an idea of which agents represent work like yours, and prepare a checklist of all that is required to submit your work. Most agents and publishers request a synopsis and the first three chapters of your novel (approximately fifty pages). Don't be tempted to send random chapters in the mistaken belief that some chapters are better than others. Your work will not be read if you do this. If the first three chapters aren't your best writing, work on them until they are!

Synopsis

Your synopsis is an outline, an overview of your novel and an important selling document. It's an essential piece of writing because it acts as an introduction, a guide to your novel. It should tell agents and publishers everything they need to know, so that they can make a decision about whether or not to accept the book for publication.

Nathan Bransford, a literary agent with Curtis Brown Ltd in New York, offers three extremely useful points which should help when you're writing a synopsis:

- It needs to cover all of the major characters and major plot points.
- It needs to make the work come alive.
- Do not under any circumstances tell your synopsis in the following manner: '….and then this happened, and then that happened…'

You should aim for a balance between covering the plot and the characters but also conveying the spirit and tone of the book and smoothing over gaps between the major plot points you describe.

I must admit that I find writing a synopsis almost as taxing as writing a novel and you may feel the same. However, it's a skill you need to develop as it's not unheard of for an agent or publisher to read only the synopsis before deciding then and there if it's worth progressing to reading the sample chapters. I strongly urge all my students to conquer the art of writing a synopsis as very few agents will be prepared to spend many hours reading through a manuscript without knowing the basic outline of the novel.

Carole Blake of literary agency Blake Friedman reinforces this in her book *From Pitch to Publication*: "I'm going to stick to my guns and say that I won't read chapters from a potential new client unless I also have a synopsis." She says a synopsis should provide answers to the following key questions:

- Whose story is it?
- What do they want, and what stops them from getting it?
- How do they get it?

Your synopsis should highlight your central character. Be clear about who they are. Explain what they want and what stops them from getting it. What obstacles are in their path? Is your character able to get what he sets out to achieve? Focus on the action because agents and editors want to know what happens more than the way people are feeling, unless what they're feeling triggers something spectacular.

In a previous chapter I've urged you to show and not tell in your novel, but the reverse is true of a synopsis. You need to tell the agent or publisher what your book is all about – the beginning, the middle and the end. Lay out the plot in the order you have written it. If you are using flashbacks, identify them in the novel, at the stage where they will appear. Bring in subplots where they reflect, develop or echo the themes of the main story or if they're a real departure and not in the sample chapters you will be including with your synopsis. If, in your novel, a cascade of frogs arrive in a sleepy French town, the agent needs to know about it. Leave out minor characters unless they appear in the sample chapters you're sending or if you feel they're crucial to the main plot.

Show how the story develops, including the theme as well as the plot, getting close to the resolution but, in my view, don't give away exactly how it's resolved (for example, 'he knows what he must do', but without saying what). You should aim to hold something back, but still give a feel of what kind of ending the book has, because an agent will need to know that you can resolve the plot and finish the book satisfactorily. If they don't have all the information, they can't make a decision about the commercial viability of taking on your novel. They need to be sure they can sell it!

Writing a good synopsis is a challenge and you may find that if you began your preparations for this novel with a plan, a list of chapters and what happens in each chapter, you can use that as a skeleton for your synopsis. That's assuming of course, that you have stuck to the original plan.

When writing a synopsis, aim for no more than two pages. I don't think you'll be penalized if it's any longer but two pages should be enough.

You should exact the same high standard for your synopsis as the one you've achieved with your novel. It might take three or four attempts to put together a competent synopsis. Invest in the time, because it is a crucial part of the whole writing process. For my part, I write a rough draft and then re-write it, taking my time, and I'll continue until I'm satisfied with the result.

The following synopsis is for my first novel *Missing Nancy* and might be helpful to you as a guide:

The novel charts the lives of Jonathan, an 'almost twelve'-year-old boy and that of his maternal grandfather, Frank, who is 79. Nancy was Jonathan's grandmother and Frank's wife and she died before the novel begins.

Jonathan lives with his divorced mother, Nina, and baby brother, Sebastian, and is aware of the ill-feeling between Nina and Frank. He tries to protect his mother and her laid back approach to motherhood, defending her against Frank's scathing criticism.

Although Nancy is dead, her influence is still keenly felt by the family. Nina apologises to her when she is unable to communicate with Frank. Jonathan talks to her, gaining comfort from the fact that she always promised to look after him.

When, following the end of yet another disastrous relationship, Nina decides to travel to France on a camping holiday with the two boys, Jonathan keeps in contact with Frank, telling him of their plans and how well Nina is coping and that the holiday is proving to be a success. He has been aware that Frank believed the holiday would be a disaster.

During the trip, Sebastian goes missing and, in the ensuing drama, Jonathan phones his father, Chris, telling him what had happened. Chris arrives in France, determined that Jonathan return to the UK with him. Nina reacts badly to the suggestion and the carefully structured, once happy holiday, implodes.

Back in the UK Frank is coping silently with as yet undiagnosed osteoarthritis and osteoporosis, doggedly ignoring the pain he is in. He too talks to Nancy, often comparing the way she brought up their son, Chris, with the more slapdash approach that Nina employs.

Frank's memories of his happy marriage are exposed as sham by Nina's disclosure to Chris during an argument.

When, following an accident, Frank is admitted to hospital, the family return to the UK and realise that, by their actions, they have let Nancy down. Eventually a solution is worked out and they are all aware of the impact that Nancy still has on their family life.

Character Biographies

Some agents and publishers like to see a biography of each main character. They may need these to inform them of past events in the character's life that might have a bearing on their behaviour in the novel. If you submit these biographies, focus on your character's appearance, how old they are at the beginning of the novel, their relationship to other characters, their job and personality traits.

Character biographies can act as a supplement to your synopsis, which can then outline the plot of the novel without being cluttered up with character details.

If you've already written character biographies as discussed at the beginning of this book, you might find that you only need to tighten the writing, perhaps slimming it down to a paragraph per character as you bring it up to date with what your character has done in the novel. The aim is to have a succinct but informative package to send to a prospective agent or publisher together with your sample chapters.

Covering letter

Finally, you'll need to write a succinct but informative one page accompanying letter. In this letter say what your day job is and certainly if you've reached a position of authority, mention that too. If you're a parent of five children under eight years old, writing in the early hours of the morning, put that in your letter. Include information about how long you've been writing, whether you've had any writing success and if you're attending writing classes. You're aiming for a suggestion of determination combined with a real love of writing.

Agents expect to see someone who demonstrates resolve and, importantly, is planning a career in writing. Age at this stage is not important if you consider that Mary Wesley was 72 when her first novel was published and she subsequently published a whole series of books. Both agents and publishers will be looking for writers with potential who are willing to write a second, third, fourth novel.

Your letter should be businesslike and professional, beautifully typed, with your address and contact details clearly visible. Under no circumstances write your letter in green ink, put smiley faces on the page, or add witty one-liners. I know of one student who wrote on his letter, 'You've read the rest, now read the best'. It is sufficient to say that his manuscript was rejected.

Steer clear of telling the agent or publisher that your family has read it and thinks your novel is wonderful. That carries no weight at all, other than describing your family as well meaning. Always enclose a stamped addressed envelope, large enough to contain your three chapters; if you don't, the chances are that your manuscript won't be returned to you.

Don't inform the agent that you will be ringing him at the end of the week to discuss your submission – your manuscript is of the utmost importance to you, but low down on the list of the agent's priorities. Finally, allow time. Don't make contact until two or three weeks have elapsed, and when you do telephone, remain polite and simply ask if the manuscript has been received.

Covering letter essentials:

DO:
* Keep to one page
* Be succinct but informative
* Include your contact details
* Enclose a large SAE

DON'T:
* Make jokes
* Make wild claims for your work
* Say your family love the novel

Approaching an Agent or Publisher

So you've prepared synopsis, character biographies and you have a fantastic covering letter. Who should you send this fabulous package off to – an agent, or a publisher?

▪ Agents

My recommendation would be to seek an agent first before trying the publishers. An agent will act for you, seek out the best deal, approach all the publishing houses on your behalf. When searching for an agent, look to see the names of their existing clients. If you've written a science fiction novel, look at the authors' names and if none of them has written science fiction, the chances are that that particular agent will not be able to help you.

When checking through the list of agents' names and addresses, read through their submission guidelines. If they clearly state that they will accept no email submissions, do not be tempted to send your work in via email in the mistaken belief that once they've read your novel, the end will justify the means. Once again, it will mean that your work will not be read.

It might be worth while to ring a literary agency to tell them about your novel, sounding them out before you submit your manuscript. They will be able to tell you if your novel is something they would be interested in. If not, they may tell you who to contact instead. If you know of someone who has an agent, talk to them, tell them about your book and ask if their agent would be willing to see it.

One word of warning – few reputable agencies will ask for a reading fee. My advice would be to discount any who do. An agent should make their money by selling your work and taking a commission (usually 10-15%), not charging you to read it.

When you submit your manuscript, it will join others

on what is called 'the slush pile'. Literary agent Carole Blake explains, "We receive at least twenty unsolicited manuscripts a day and, to be honest, we are looking for reasons to say no." She does, however, go on to say, "I still get such excitement from a really new voice writing something that grabs my attention."

※ Single submission or multiples?
In the past, authors would submit their manuscripts to only one agent at a time, waiting for a response from one before approaching another. However, the length of time it can take for a response means that the goalposts have shifted somewhat, and it is now perfectly acceptable to submit your novel to more than one agent at the same time.

It is only when an agent has asked to see the complete manuscript that they expect exclusivity. You may send a synopsis and three chapters out to several agents, but remember that only one agent at a time should have your complete manuscript.

※ What happens to your submission?
It is my understanding that in many agencies a junior member of staff reads through the submitted chapters before notifying a senior literary agent if the manuscript has attracted their attention. You may then get a phone call asking for the rest of the novel to be posted.

The literary agent will then read the whole thing, and decide whether they think they can sell it and whether you as a novelist are marketable. If the answers to both those questions is a 'yes', then you'll get a phone call asking you to go to the agent's offices to discuss what happens next. This is the moment at which you should feel very proud!

An agent's job is to approach publishers and try to sell your novel. This can be a long process, and the agent might have to contact a great many publishing houses on your behalf in an attempt to persuade them to publish your book. It's not a foregone conclusion that the agent will immediately find a publisher. It is certainly not unknown for an agent, no matter how hard they try, to be unable to find a publisher willing to take you on, and even after the agent has found a publishing house willing to take your book on, it's not all plain sailing. A lot depends on the state of the market – styles change and books go in and out of fashion. However, if the genre that you have written in is in demand, the publication could be handled promptly to take advantage of the market.

Publishers

Some writers approach publishing houses directly, finding an agent to represent them through the negotiations afterwards. With a publishing deal already secure, the search for an agent should be markedly easier.

Look for the names of publishers not only in the *Writers' Handbook*, but on the spines of books you have at home or you find in book shops.

The format for presenting your work to publishers is the same as that for agents. Supply them with a covering letter, a synopsis, and the first three chapters of your novel.

The process your manuscript will go through is similar to that with an agent. A junior member of staff will read your submission, and if they like it they'll pass it on to a senior editor. You may then get a phone call asking for the rest of the novel. The complete manuscript will then appear at a meeting when marketing will be discussed, whether the publisher can expect healthy sales and whether you as a novelist are marketable. If the answers to all those questions is 'yes' then you will get a phone call to discuss what happens next. This is where you may like to enlist the services of a literary agent to steer you through contract negotiations.

Listed in the two writers' handbooks is a list of small

publishers. Don't discount them on the basis of size alone. Contact them by letter or email asking if they would be interested in seeing your work. If the reply is favourable, then send in your submission. Small publishers can sometimes act more quickly than a larger organisation and at least one book on the list of small publisher Tindall Street Press has been short listed for the Booker Prize.

Dealing with rejection

Nearly all first time novelists will hear the thump as their returning manuscript lands on the doormat. Unless you're very lucky (and luck is as important as talent), rejection is part of a writer's life. Don't despair. Apparently, Ian Fleming received nearly seventy rejection letters and J. K. Rowling was turned down by twenty agents.

Alongside your returned manuscript, you might find an apology from the agent expressing an interest in your future novels. Take heart from this; agents are busy people and they rarely bother to say something this unless they mean it.

Bear in mind that your novel will be read initially by one person, that does not mean that your work is no good, it simply means that your manuscript did not appeal to that person. Novels are subjective, not everyone likes the same thing. If your novel comes back from one agent, send it to another. Keep a careful check on who you are sending your work to, so there is no chance that you will send the manuscript to the same agent twice.

And finally, don't dwell on the rejections. Simply send the novel out again. Make sure that each time you send your work out, it looks pristine, even if this means printing off new letters or a fresh synopsis.

Self Publishing

With developments in print on demand technology, self

publishing is becoming an increasingly popular option for many writers, particularly so for those who've written something that's of personal or niche interest that a mainstream publisher wouldn't be interested in taking it on.

Self publishing means, quite literally, that you publish yourself. Many writers find this extremely liberating, because they can make all the decisions about what goes into the book, how it looks, what features on the jacket, and how it's marketed. However, that can be a lot of work for one person to take on. A self publisher needs to become an expert in editing, typesetting, proofreading, book jacket design, project management, publishing administration, printing, marketing and promotions.

Some writers juggle these roles successfully and have great fun doing so.

Others don't want to be publishers – they want to get on with writing their next book and so engage other experts to handle the publishing side for them. These experts are called 'publishing services providers' or 'self publishing companies' and they'll be happy to steer you through the publishing process.

It is worth remembering that when choosing to self publish or buy in professional publishing services, you should not make your decision on the basis of cost alone. You're entering a crowded and competitive market place and with that in mind, your work must be professionally edited, typeset and designed and then printed to the highest quality you can afford. The book you end up with must look like mainstream books on a similar subject. If your intention is to sell your book, then it really is in your best interests to achieve the polished appearance of any book stacked on the shelves of high street booksellers.

Finally

I do hope that this book has been of some help to you. My one intention has been to demystify the art of novel writing and make the project seem less daunting. It was never my intention to tell you how to write – that can't be taught – but instead to focus on ways to make the writing process achievable. I graduated from the University of Glamorgan with an MPhil in Writing, having learnt various techniques and methods. Armed with these new skills, my first novel was published in 2008 and I now write regularly for a leading women's magazine. It was not an easy path. There were obstacles, rejections and a great many times when I found myself wondering whether it was all worth it…

But it was – and I hope it will be for you too.

Carolyn Lewis
Bristol, 2010